Akashic Records

Unlock the Secret Key to Manifesting the Law of Attraction

(The World's Most Comprehensive Guide to Opening the Akashic Records)

Adam Reaves

Published By **Oliver Leish**

Adam Reaves

Akashic Records: Unlock the Secret Key to Manifesting the Law of Attraction (The World's Most Comprehensive Guide to Opening the Akashic Records)

ISBN   978-1-998769-10-0

No part of this guidebook shall be reproduced in any form without permission in writing from the publisher except in the case of brief quotations embodied in critical articles or reviews.

Legal & Disclaimer

The information contained in this ebook is not designed to replace or take the place of any form of medicine or professional medical advice. The information in this ebook has been provided for educational & entertainment purposes only.

The information contained in this book has been compiled from sources deemed reliable, and it is accurate to the best of the Author's knowledge; however, the Author cannot guarantee its accuracy and validity and cannot be held liable for any errors or omissions. Changes are periodically made to this book. You must consult your doctor or get professional medical advice before using any of the suggested remedies, techniques, or information in this book.

Upon using the information contained in this book, you agree to hold harmless the Author

TABLE OF CONTENTS

Chapter 1: The Akashic World

Akashic World

"The word Akashic record was invented during the late 19th century. It was a way of conceptualizing the notion that humans might be able (or already had the capability) to access the record of human experiences that date back to the beginning of the species, or even the Earth. According to some theorists, this sort of knowledge wasn't limited to the Earth as well as our solar system. Rather, every planet had its own library of knowledge that was available to people living who resided in these places.

The akashic theories came out in a time where philosophers and other geniuses were contemplating the world's changing or was overloaded with information. European nations were experiencing an era of Industrial Revolution, which brought significant social changes and also a swell in the changes that was already underway. With the rise of education. People all over Europe and all over the world were becoming more familiar with the different languages and cultures of the East and making use of this knowledge to develop the theories of their own.

The idea of the akashic is intriguing as, even though it appears to be linked to ideas that originate from the East specifically, from The Indian subcontinent as well as in the Near East, it was evidently an European thought-stream that utilized a rationalization to these ideas that were hundreds many years old. What do we mean this time? This idea of the eternal nature of time or of the cycle of history repeating itself in a sequence of creation and destruction governed by Vedic gods, which is a key concept in Hinduism and Buddhism, was not novel. These ideas were at most 2000 years old, but they were not known to the majority of Europeans.

European thought was dominating by Western Christian thinking, which was primarily based on the concept of creation and did not address the notion of time. In fact, Christian theory approached time as something that would come to an end when the universe was destroyed. This was radically distinct from the practices of various Southern Asian and Near Eastern religions, which we could consider mysterious. They did not just perceive the notion of time differently and believed that humans might be able of interacting to time in a manner that would have puzzled the minds of many Europeans.

The exposure of a new educated group from European minds to a variety of these cultures as a result of the translation of works such as The Bhagavad Ghita, which is a crucial Vedic test. The first translation known to English took place in 1785 followed by another one that was influential in 1849. The last translation was likely to have occurred at a time when a lot of people were capable of reading the text. The system of public education as well as the development of university education across a variety of languages would not only made the translation more accessible, but also created interest in a broader audience.

Vedic practices of Brahmanism has influenced, among other things, Helen Blavatsky, the creator of the modern day Theosophy movement, and is as one of the intriguing aspects of the concept. Born to an Russian family of aristocratic origin She traveled around all over the world, and was able to express her interest in spirituality. She went across Egypt, Tibet, and to India in which she seemed to be able to see the profound relationship with Buddhism and Brahmanism and saw the latter as a genuine the descendant from

Brahmanic tradition as opposed to the modern day Hinduism.

Blavatsky she sometimes claimed to be a Buddhist She introduced the concept of akasha to the spiritual movement. She believed it was a form of life energy which was further developed by two other key individuals within the theosophic movement. Henry Steel Olcott and Alfred Percy Sinnett. The two writers also made a clear connection with Buddhism along with the Akashic notion which became a major part of the theosophic tradition. Olcott particularly believed that the concept of akasha was in line with the Buddha's concept of interconnectedness and indestructibility. Akasha was a kind or permanent document that was able to be read and accessed by anyone in the quest for awakening.

Akasha is an Sanskrit term, Sanskrit being the language of the Vedic period of Ancient Indian history. Some consider it as the oldest language in the Indo-European language family, Sanskrit is related to many languages from the European continent as well as in the Near East, including Persian, Greek, Latin, and many more. Through the use of terms borrowed from earlier religions and connecting them to old spiritual and linguistic movements, Blavatsky created a movement that appeared older and more grounded in the past than it actually was.

The theosophic revolution, although it had many followers during the 19th century, was in fact a brand revolutionary movement. It was influential since many of the writers and political theorists in during the 20th centuries were influenced by theosophical ideas as well as other similar movements. How exactly does theosophy work? you might be thinking. Theosophy is an spiritual doctrine that focuses on the concept of a universal brotherhood among all mankind. While Blavatsky herself wrote texts that more detailed her views, theosophy is not believed to provide a clear set of beliefs to which followers are required to adhere.

One of the most intriguing aspects of theosophy for many people is the faith in ancient civilizations from Atlantis as well as Lemuria. Greek belief in Atlantis as a civilization which was buried beneath the ocean prior to the historical period, and was the subject of intense speculation among Blavatsky as well as others Theosophists. Blavatsky as well as other theosophists didn't believe in the historical accounts that put Atlantis as a human, historical context that earlier writers did. In the eyes of Blavatsky, Atlantis and Lemuria were viewed as the sites that were "root races" with cosmic roots.

Blavatsky was of the opinion that first roots were energy However, she also believed that Atlanteans were decrepit and savage, resulting in their continent being swept away into the ocean. Lemuria was believed to be continuing for a long time in South Pacific, a theory which is not completely untrue. Modern science suggests the possibility that New Zealand and other islands in the Pacific might be remnants of a continent that was lost, and there's the physical proof of an ancient civilization New Zealand, although archaeological exploration hasn't been initiated because of the desire to keep what secrets there are just as secrets.

Theosophical doctrine doesn't require certain beliefs however, those writings by Helena Blavatsky, Henry Olcott and others have established the foundational beliefs that a lot of people in the movement adhere to. The early theosophists and their followers later on were captivated by the mystical concepts they attributed to Indian religions as well as Ancient Egypt. They considered themselves to be the being the heirs to ancient wisdom and believed that certain discoveries from the past supported their belief system.

Geologists, archaeologists along with other scientists and researchers discovered that the suppositions of the past were confirmed through archaeological evidence and some people such as Blavatsky believed that there were additional theories which could be valid. If it was true that the city of Troy was real, and the sites that are mentioned in The Iliad were true, why wouldn't Atlantis also be real? By combining their knowledge of the spiritual world and elements of ancient religions, they were able to establish a culture that has allowed people to access ancient wisdom in ways that were previously thought to be impossible in the Christian world in which all things were believed to conform to the strict rules.

Is theosophy a new tradition or an Old One?

The idea of Akashic records and the theosophical traditions and anthroposophy it is connected to are not new ideas however, they are based on the belief that humans have powers that have been constant since the beginning of our existence on earth. Theosophists from the beginning combined various styles to form an ideology that stretches all the way to the very beginning of the time. Their beliefs were a blend of Platonic philosophy and the historical facts with beliefs that came from outside of Europe and were based in Asia as well as North Africa, and which the majority of Europeans were at the time getting exposed to.

Theosophists believed that their religion was not a new concept however, they believed that it was an ancient tradition that had roots on Buddhism, Brahmanism, and other religions. One could argue that it was a spiritual practice that was always there but was only beginning to be appreciated during the early 19th century. Theosophical beliefs attracted a large number of adherents as it became newly established in the latter part of the 19th century. This number would only increase throughout the 20th century when certain people began to view the latest developments in science as proof of the validity of theosophical thought.

The 20th century's scientific theories. century

Physical theories that address questions about the origins of our universe caused a mess in the waters of our understanding of the universe. Even though physics and other sciences try to make the world accessible by establishing rules that every living thing within the universe is bound but these theories seem to open doors that they shut. When we discover how the universe came into existence with black holes that are which are so far away that they're already dead when their light hits us, we ask what the roots of the ideas that constitute the foundation of much of Western thought actually be a good explanation for the world we are living in.

Physics's most innovative minds may have, which might be at first glance, proposed theories that appear to suggest that certain theories promoted by the movements of theosophy and anthroposophy may not be as crazy as the scientific community would like to claim. Physics researchers, particularly in the latter half during the second half of 20th century began to doubt whether we knew our universe in the same way than we thought we could.

A renowned and well-known thinkers during the 20th century was Stephen Hawking. Some consider him to be controversial, Hawking was a director at the University of Cambridge's Centre of Theoretical Cosmology. Stephen Hawking pondered a lot of ideas about the origins of human existence, as well as the universe's nature However, the majority of his research and theories were based around two main areas which were black holes and an alternate universes.

The black hole an elongated vortex that has the ability to pull matter through gravitational forces. It is impossible to escape the pull of gravity from the black hole. Hawking was in a position to illuminate the phenomenon that is affecting the universe by revealing that universe-wide structure emits radiation. The application of Hawking's theories that are most relevant to the study about Akashic records is the one of alternate universes, which are also known as parallel universes.

Hawking believed that there were parallel universes. He also claimed that physicists were near to proving that there are alternative universes. This is significant due to a variety of reasons. First , Hawking died in the last few days, was among the most well-known theorists of theoretical physics. His ideas were influenced by the belief that cosmological ideas weren't at all far-fetched and could actually be proved by the physicists. It is crucial to remember this because critics of cosmological thinking frequently claim that they do not have a basis in any evidence from science.

Additionally, the concept of alternate universes isn't too far from the idea in that of the Akashic records, even though it takes the concept from a different perspective. The Akashic record is founded on the fundamental Buddhist and Brahmanic notion of a record of experiences shared by anyone who has opened their minds can access. The concept is based on the notion the notion that time can be a multifaceted variable that doesn't conform to the linear concept that many Westerners are accustomed to when they think of time.

The Western mind sees time in terms of present, past, and the future. The linear nature of time is evident with the past occurring before the present. The moment of time we are in is in the present, whereas the future is clearly something that happens in the future, and appears to be escaping us. What is the case if the universe were an energy structure that time wasn't distinct into separate entities, with one being within one place in "past" and one within"the future. "future."

A large portion of Vedic faith is based on the notion of the cycles of creation and destruction which is tightly tied to the cycle of time however, it also suggests a more sophisticated concept of the time cycle than is typically found for Western culture. Western mind. Vedic texts talk about God Brahma who creates for the creation's purpose. The millions of years that humans live are just a single day for Brahma who floods the earth , and then creates it again, binding every living thing to cycles of birth and the loss of life, death, and renewal, all a as part of the all-encompassing order.

The various religions in South Asia approached Brahma differently This is crucial to theosophy's philosophies and the concept of akashic records , to which the movement is connected. Brahma was a god of great importance in the earlier Vedic tradition, but not as important in the modern Hinduism. There aren't many temples be dedicated to him in India of the present, since gods such as Kali, Vishnu, Shiva and others are much more well-known. However, Brahma was and remains the central figure of Buddhism and it was Buddhist tradition that may have had the most influence on the early theosophists.

This Buddhist and Brahmanic concepts are crucial for akashic records as well as their understanding because they considered the energy of life or as something unbreakable, something that was quite different of what was known as the Russian Orthodox religion that Helena Blavatsky was born into in which her felt a connection even during the last few days of her existence. The practices in Buddhism and Brahmanism gave way to a realm that was much older than what the Christian tradition claimed. In fact, this world was so ancient that it was almost inconceivable and this particular moment was just one of the many moments in a river that ran extremely far.

What if the archives of the energy generated in the world, energy that is represented by life or death and rebirth, many of them through the ages What if all of the records could be accessed? This was the concept behind The Akashic record that early theosophists such as Helena Blavatsky believed, and it was in fact tied to the beliefs of ancient South Asian religions. In actual fact, Blavatsky took these ideas to the next level, by incorporating her own view of Cosmology into the brand new philosophy she was constructing.

In fact, this main reason for South Asian influence combined with the flavors of other traditions like the ones in Ancient Egypt as well as Greece may have brought an unintended blessing to the tradition of theosophy and theosophy. The critics argue that this drawing from multiple sources with the emergence of new ideas in the 19th century made an unsubstantiated pseudoscience that did not have its roots on any actual facts. On the other hand those who adhere to these traditions argue that drawing inspiration from ancient the traditions that were many thousands of years old, and linking them to new information from the future, they resulted in a belief system which might have been more effective than its predecessors.

What you can learn from this conversation are the following concepts concerning Akashic records:

* Akashic records are a record of the lives of people who been alive and gone to the grave

* Akashic records are stored on an ethereal level that is accessible by the mind

* Akashic records are part of an intricate cosmological picture with various regions of the universe possessing their own archives that are accessible to the living beings who reside in those areas.

* The akasha's rites that are linked to theosophy and anthroposophy are derived from concepts derived from Brahmanism, Buddhism, and other ancient traditions.

* Old traditions were merged with modern cosmological and spiritual concepts to form the new movement known as theosophy in the 19th century.

* While natural science has been viewed by many as these ideas as not being based on proof that is derived from using the method of scientific inquiry, recent theories have given credibility to a number of these theories.

* The idea of the theoretical physical concept of alternate universes as well as the complexity of time is similar to the way theosophy views the universe and the concept of time.

* A large number of physicists in the present believe they are getting close to concluding the existence of alternate universes. Perhaps it's not that different from the ethereal space where the akashic record compendium exists. It is an archive that the minds of the earth can access.

In the following chapters, you'll discover more about how science has confirmed some of the most fundamental theories regarding akashic records. Also, you will acquire practical understanding of how to gain access to Akashic records by tapping on the memories of the entire universe that exists in the ethereal realm of all the lives that have been lived in our particular part of the universe.

Chapter 2: Evidence For Akashic Records

If you are not familiar with the concept that are associated with Akashic record and feeling curious about about the implications of this kind of knowledge could provide them with is bound to wonder whether there is any actual evidence to support these records . It is not your intention to smear the beliefs system. If you're here, it's likely that some experiences you have had convinced you that as humans are able to access information that is not governed by the rules of science Perhaps knowledge that comes from our ancestors or information that seems to originate from supernatural sources.

People in their daily lives might experience the sensation of having dreams that appear to have occurred in the past or even in the future. People have dreams that are waking or other visions which appear to originate from an else"s mind or one's own mind. was in the past or even in the future. Certain people have been able to see clairvoyants or have had experiences of having clairvoyant knowledge. Many people have reported that in this world which seems to be in a state of chaos, they feel more connected to other people and get the feeling of being of other people, possibly one that is more powerful than it ever was before.

However, our modern sciences would want us to believe that everything we see can be explained with the rules in our science textbooks, and that we need to only be able to believe the things we can see with our own eyes, a lot of people believe that there are things that they have a sense of and see, but without the aid of their eyes. Many ancient religions, and especially ones that include meditation as an integral component is based on the idea that knowledge can be acquired through the mind, and also the capacity for minds to connect because of their interconnected nature of human beings.

The current trends in religion and culture have created a culture which is disconnected from nature. Many of us have experienced this. We are constantly reading of global climate change, the rising levels of water all over the world, and the destruction of a vast number of animal and plant species across the globe. We are bombarded with pictures of natural disasters, catastrophes which get more severe every year. Superstorms and hurricanes are becoming more frequent in various areas of the world, and will continue to increase in frequency as the melting of the polar ice caps.

Science informs we that they are issues of science and have scientific solutions. It could be so however, many people believe that there is an emotional connection to the earth and consider that there are things that science hasn't been able to explain, or has not yet managed to clarify. In the first chapter, you were introduced to in the beginning of this chapter, scientists have started to accept that certain cosmological or spiritual beliefs aren't as distant from science as they had been thought to be. The notion that science is not keeping the pace of knowledge that people with a lack of science (or less than that we do) could have derived and is easily felt by people.

A interesting trend in Western sciences and historiography is that what we think we know in the present can be proven to be incorrect, putting historians and scientists in a position of having to review the information they have or believe they knew. We learn the fact that American Indians have been living in the Western Hemisphere much longer than we believed due to the discovery of bones along the West Coast of South America.

Western history suggests that the island of Polynesia were settled longer after oral stories that was told to the indigenous people from Hawaii as well as New Zealand. Western history claims that the indigenous peoples of Polynesia never made it to the shores from North or South America. This is the only official history of the books, however, cultural similarities and the existence of certain species of plants suggest that these islands might be settled for thousands of years and traded with people who lived along the coast or perhaps participated in exchanges of population.

The scientific community has discovered that human beings could be much older than we believed and have lived on a variety of continents for millennia. These ideas are being confirmed by fossil records. Theories of continents that sank into the ocean, which were dismissed by historians as being completely false have been proven to be true at all. Today, the evidence suggests that there could have been antiquated civilizations that existed in the Pacific civilizations, which were thousands of years old are discarded even in the light of astonishing new discoveries like a massive wall of masonry discovered located in New Zealand, an area which some theosophists believe could have been part of the planet of Lemuria.

Science has looked at what they consider to be the inconsistent and unsubstantiated theories of theosophy as well as anthroposophy with suspicion, and keeping certain facts from the public eye. The people who lived during Ancient Egypt and the Near East were able to comprehend a complex view about the stars possibly more complex than the one we are today, and without the use of the tools we use in science or "scientific information". According to some, when we built these pyramids in Giza in the present, we wouldn't be able to construct them with the precision of astronomy and precision of Ancient Egyptians.

How could this be? What could be the cause of the world being not scientific? In other words, how can the information that was derived from different methods that the scientific method be proven to be more precise or as comprehensive as information we can get from our computers that are high-powered as well as sophisticated telescopes and microscopes? What source did this information come from?

This is among the areas where akashic recordings are a factor. If human beings are able to access what many consider to be an ancestral knowledge, or a memory bank that is derived from the memories of the collective mind of human beings before us and the human mind will be able to access information without the need of computers, microscopes telescopes, satellites and other such. Theosophists from the beginning addressed these issues by presenting views on the intricate cosmic picture that we live.

A lot of people are attracted to theosophy based on their personal experiences. The evidence of the existence of akashic records is plentiful and creates an assortment of different perspectives regarding theosophy. In reality, evidence from anecdotes of what people believe about their own experiences as personal is the basis of what early theosophists likely based their theories of their early years on. Individuals like Blavatsky and Olcott could have gotten some of their knowledge from their personal experiences. That's what brought them into the realm of spiritual studies at the beginning.

A typical anecdote many people have in Akashic documents is the basic sensation of having access an area of knowledge which could not be acquired through "ordinary" methods. A person may meet somebody and already have information about the person. One could have information about the history of their family without being informed. Clairvoyant experiences that show one person is able to be able to make accurate claims about the future or past of another individual are the most commonly used "anecdotal evidence" suggested to prove that there are Akashic records as well as the accessibility of them.

In spite of the usual experiences that could draw individuals to the spiritual world where akashic records play an important role, the proponents of these fields caution that there is a distinction between perceptions of the mind that are not supported by reality and the actual facts or records, which originate from a spiritual realm. Theosophists believe that anyone who is truly interested in the occult will be able to differentiate between what has actually come from the akashic recording (on the realm of the ethereal) as well as subjective, substantive perceptions that could or might not be accurate. Sometimes you sense something about someone, but it might be just an accident or a feeling.

The ability to discern is derived from experiences of people, and if you've got enough experience with others, you may be able to draw accurate predictions regarding the people you know. This is with no access to the Akashic record in the manner believed by spiritualists within the schools of theosophy as well as theosophy. How can one differentiate the subjective perception from the fact of a document that results by accessing the archive of both past and future knowledge and experiences?

Theosophists have suggested that this is a result of experiences. Unexperienced people is unable to tell the difference between an intuitional sense or having accessed an akashic recording. A person who is familiar with the spiritual realm might have a better idea about whether or not another person is likely to have accessed an akashic file however, even this may not always be accurate. Certain people might have access to Akashic records with no formal education, indicating either the gift of a native or a tradition passed down through generations with being part of an endowed ancestral group.

A person whose mind is in opposition to non-scientific theories of knowledge is likely to not be able to draw information from an akashic recording. The mind of the spiritual is a mind that is awakened by meditation or suffering, or a deep compassion for those around them, is open to having access to Akashic records, more so than a mind that holds to rigid views that deny the existence of these forms of knowledge or shared experiences. As we've discussed earlier, those who are enlightened can gain access to Akashic records due to the fact that their minds are open to the universality of experience that is a part of life on earth.

Akashic Records and the Buddhist Concept of Karma

People who have access to the akashic records can tap into the experiences and dreams for all humanity who have lived their lives on Earth. It is a karmic event since it is supported by the fundamental the interconnectedness of humans and the rest in the kingdom of animals. Karma symbolizes the concept of doing. It is the cause and the effect connection between our individual as well as collective actions and the impact they have on other people and us. Karma is connected to the notion of samsara also known as samsara, a Sanskrit word that refers to the possibility of a future world that wanders and the cyclical nature of Rebirth which is the basis of Buddhist beliefs.

Karma is usually thought of on an individual level, describing the good or bad actions of an individual and the impact that they have on the life of that individual. However, even in the most basic notions of spirituality the individual cause and effect is connected to the global causes and consequences. Each cause has an impact on an individual since we all are connected. This means that the individual causes affects other causes and has the resultant effect being passed on to the individual, all of which is a fundamental equilibrium in the world we live in.

A key concept to be noted in this regard for the benefit of the reader as an integral part of the spiritual journey as well as their attempt to understand the universe and how to interact to it notion of the word dharma. The term refers to a correct or ethical way of life but it's not something which has a literal meaning in the majority of Western languages. There is a sense of abstraction in dharma that may cause individuals to grasp. Dharma is often a reference to a collective method of living, of interaction with other people and is a key concept in a variety of Eastern religions.

Dharma is significant due to the belief that as the earth grows older and is near to its end, at a minimum before Brahma eliminates the world and makes another one (in some religions) The global dharma becomes less important. People are irritable, insensitive and cruel. The collective karma of the entire world could be described as having an imbalance. This is merely in order to bring back the idea of cyclicality that is always present within Eastern religions, and to the notion that karma is an element of collective.

The argument has been put forth that we are living in a time of diminished dharma. Some people believe that the planet is set to destroy itself. This could be the reason why certain people feel a greater feeling of interconnectedness currently. It could be that they are responding to a feeling of threat. This activates their natural ability to access Akashic records, and leading them to seek out studying spirituality to enhance their capabilities or connect to others.

One of the most important aspects of karma that theosophists have been actively absorbing is that of desire. It is the desires of Man which lead to deeds or actions, and those actions playing in the cause-and-effect relationship between the karma. According to the Brihadaranyanka Upanishad which is a Vedic text that is a significant text in Hinduism It is said that man"s desire is the catalyst for his desire, which in the end leads to a deed, an act that ultimately produces an effect that is on the desire of the individual. Theosophists viewed as the Akashic record as containing the past lives of people and their wishes as a kind of collective karma, or the dharma that the energy forms that humans are made up of.

The idea of karma is more complicated when we consider the notion that a lot of theosophists believe that the dharma and karma concepts do not just apply to human beings, but to all within the realm of animals. The experiences of all of the creatures on earth constitute a key element of the concept of karma within theosophic traditions.

It might seem difficult to some people to comprehend the significance of other creatures to our individual Karma (or for that matter, to the Akashic record, for that matter) However, it is founded on the belief that certain kinds of life exist in an enlightened state which means that a karmic cause effect relationship may be established between a human and another animal even though it might not be between animals and plants like a plant, for example.

We have discussed the concept of karma and the evidence of akashic records in order to help readers make connections between what might be a brand new concept (that of Akashic records) and what they might already be familiar with. A Akashic recording is collective type of energy that is interconnected in a sense, much in the same way as the concept of karma works. Therefore, we can describe the theosophist's view of Karma as follows:

*The Akashic recording is the repository of the experiences and dreams of higher-life forms in the earth.

* The akashic records consists of the real experiences of human beings from the very beginning of humankind which can be opened by the mind.

* The akashic records contain the karmic relations (desires wills, wills, deeds and the results) humans dating all the way back to the beginning of time.

The Akashic record includes the actions and desires of the members of the animal kingdom dating from the beginning of time.

Chapter 3: Accessing Akashic Records

Theosophists of the past believed that there existed people in their own time who were accessing what they believed were Akashic records without realizing of what they were doing. Theosophists made specific reference to clairvoyants they believed as having the ability to tap into the energy that they believed to be identified to their belief in the Akashic record. Indeed, many different cultures around the globe had their own traditions of forecasting which had to do with the wishes of the fortune-teller or clairvoyant who could draw the energy and the energy of the person who wants their destiny to be revealed.

These types of beliefs about energy and desires were commonplace in societies which had a tradition of fortune telling like certain communities in Asia as well as The

Near East, and Eastern Europe. It could involve palm reading or reading cards, or just taking your energy the fortuneteller interacted with. We hope to introduce you to the various traditions which have relied on akashic recordings and how they've done it in the first place in introducing you to the ways you can perform similar.

The notion that clairvoyants may are able to access what consider akashic data is an interesting idea. It's not just a speculative speculation. Clairvoyance was believed to be an indication to prove the existence of an Akashic record, a proof that the akashic universe wasn't something invented by. In reality many of the first believers in theosophy were from areas where there was the practice of clairvoyance and fortune-telling. Blavatsky and others also found significant support from India in India, where the connection between theosophy's early ancestors along with Indic religions was obvious.

Blavatsky was very clear about drawing similarities among Buddhism, Brahmanism, and theosophy, but Clairvoyance was an entirely different pot of worms. Clairvoyance, also known as fortunetelling, was not founded on a specific set of principles as Buddhism or Hinduism were , and remain to this day. There were no institutions for clairvoyance, or at least not in a formal way or even officially. The practices that were taught in one culture could be completely different from the beliefs held in another. In fact, even within a particular cultural context there may be different opinions.

It is interesting to consider but is the role cosmic cosmology has played in the realm of clairvoyance as well as fortune telling. Clairvoyants rely on information such as the dates of their births, dates and ages as well as star charts, to assess the health of people as well as to predict their future.

They also make use of these data to tell people when it is a good time to engage in specific activities or to avoid other activities. Astrological information was utilized to establish a method of rigor on what seemed to be a hazy science, though how it is interpreted could have different interpretations in different various cultures.

It's not an easy issue to establish a link between the way clairvoyants utilize the astrological data as well as their knowledge of the Akashic record. It's an interesting subject to think about. The theory suggests that there is a space that contains information regarding human lives from the past and the present is accessible however it does not say little about how this information might be linked in with the stars. Certain clairvoyants might be able to utilize the information of the astrological world to access the akashic records, at least in relation to an individual.

Others clairvoyants and fortune tellers make use of cards of the Tarot. Tarot cards are believed as a new invention, which is believed by many historians to have originated mostly originated from Italian noble courts in during the latter Medieval and Renaissance times They draw from practices that are much older. In fact, the Romans had priests who were specially trained or augurs who were responsible for interpreting signals prior to deciding what decision was taken. Augurs had a variety of tools they could use to interpret these signs, from analyzing the movements of birds on a specific day, to studying the pattern of the entrails of the animal that was sacrificed.

Although the intent is not to enter into philosophical discussions however, it is interesting to think about the interaction between a specific sign and its capacity in predicting the future. From a philosophical perspective it is possible to suggest that a sign can be bridges with the aim of an augur, clairvoyant or priest, to understand the meaning of the sign. This means that the desire to be able to comprehend something or learn something could result in the action of a sign and all the components are an element of a cause and result reaction.

This is among those areas of theosophy which has been of constant interest to many because it goes back to the notion of karmic and karma forces within the Akashic record. We have discussed the ways that the Vedic texts interpret karma at the most basic level, which is the result of a desire, which results in the will of the person, and can result in an outcome. This concept was accepted by the theosophists because they believed in their Akashic document as having the desire for karmic pleasures of humans and animals , in addition to the actual actions, as we could call them.

Did augurs, priests and fortune tellers able convert their desire to interpret an indication into the creation of a sign at the very minimum create an entire sequence of events that led to the right interpretation of the sign? A majority of people would say"yes. Augurs, clairvoyants and others could be tapping the Akashic record by engaging within the spiritual process that transforms desires into actions. This could also be true for Tarot cards. A fortune-teller can make tarot cards which best align to the Akashic record details of the person who is of interest and the query being asked.

If augursand priests or psychics, fortune-tellers healers and clairvoyants have been successful in using karmic forces to access the Akashic record, there is no reason you shouldn't achieve the similar. This is an easy method to transform thoughts into action. Human beings can shape our environment with our thoughts, creating the world we live in. For some it could be as easy as thinking of someone's name and having the person call them a few seconds later. It could be a matter of deciding whether or not to embark in a specific method of doing something, and then , the universe does you a favor by generating for you a signal.

The issue of whether the data received really represents tapping into the Akashic record or not raises its ugly head once more. This is a question that theosophists of the past pondered and pondered as well as one you will have to face should you decide to tap into the Akashic record yourself. It is true that in the initial stages of this field, you might not be able to tell if you've connected to your Akashic records or not. There is a chance that you have an intuition or feel that has nothing to do with have anything to do with an Akashic record. You may also get what appears to be an indication, but it's not. It is also possible to receive a message and then miss-interpret the meaning.

The process of accessing the Akashic record, therefore, is an art that needs to be refined like all other art forms. One of the most important concepts to consider with regards to the idea that humans are able to predict the future, or even understand the past in a way that is utterly supernatural. does not come without the support of scientists. In addition to this notion of alternate universes, which Stephen Hawking and others have believed in There is also a growing epigenetics field that is poised to change our perception of human beings and their capabilities to change the course of human evolution.

The study is of the genes which could be expressed in different ways. This is a genetic trait that humans possess but may not use at the moment. Researchers have found that dolphins communicate with sonar, however they may also be able to communicate using mental methods completely different from sonar, which is what we call"telepathy. Aren't human beings also able to possess the same abilities that they haven't learned to utilize? It is not a novel idea in theosophy, as the notion that Atlanteans or Lemurians being superior to the humans are of today is a one of Atlantis concept that is embraced by theosophy.

So accessing Akashic records which we'll discuss practicalally in the next chapter, could involve the use of karmic forces to tap into the akashic record which includes the collective karmic needs. Additionally, it may lead to opening up human nature such as the ability to communicate with other people using our minds. This process can result in a complex interconnected web of wishes as well as wills and consequences all recorded on a document. However, engaging in this intricate dance could require a crucial first step: preparing your brain to be ready for the task.

Chapter 4: The Mind's Preparation To Access Akashic Records

The idea that you might be capable of accessing Akashic archives, or be already doing and are now perceptible to you. Theosophists of the past believed that humans were the energy of a particular form that had an individual and collective identity. They believed that the records of these energy forms were stored in their Akashic records. In the form of energy, not the basic material structures that science speculates about that human beings possess certain capabilities that could outshine what a mere collection of bones, skin and organs are capable of doing.

We briefly discussed the notion that humans are capable of tapping into long hidden abilities in the previous chapter. This is something that science is slowly starting to recognize, even if they're not completely on the same page with theosophical ideas regarding the soul and energy. Although you might not fully believe in the notion that all human experiences of the past and future are on a written record, a specific plane, and people who have been skilled in the field are adept at accessing this realm of ethereal energy however, the idea of the human condition in which, you are gifted with abilities you've not yet explored yet is more accessible. It may even be evident to you.

Films and books are filled with characters, referred to as "chosen ones" who are allegedly able to go beyond their human limitations to achieve feats that other people would never have dreamed of. But what if this is not abilities that only one person has and are an integral part of human potential. In the movie The Matrix, the character Neo can manipulate space around himself as well as challenge gravity's laws through his understanding of the rules of the artificial universe within which he lives.

You too can tap into your potential by knowing the rules that govern our physical environment. While your environment may appear tangible to your eyes, it's actually governed with artificial regulations as the matrix to which thought machines have tied humans too. You're just as involved in the performance of your life or an artificial one like Neo was and achieving the full potential of an individual will require you to use your brain to create the environment around you.

How do you accomplish that? This is the million-dollar question. In reality, some of you have done this. We've mentioned many instances in the book about the ways in which people could have access to the Akashic record without realizing. Some people may have an irrational mind trained to doubt the reality surrounding it, thus making you, just like Neo the neophyte, capable of breaking any "rules." The book identifies certain traits of those who have started an act of preparation for mental health.

The most important thing here is the notion of desires and thoughts that lead to the action. In the event that you think the universe is controlled by rules, and that all that exists are those scientifically explainable, this is the universe that you've created. This means that you are not in a position to gain access to the akashic record if think that the akashic record exists because it doesn't conform to scientific theories of the moment. Arguably the initial step in getting access to this Akashic record is to believe that there exists an underlying knowledge realm that is accessible through your mind.

It may appear like jumping into the dark end of the water to engage in what's often referred to in the world of literature as suspension of doubt butin reality when you read this book, you've already started the process of suspending doubt, if there was doubt to begin with. When you read this book, you're willing to accept the fact that the world wasn't so simple as you had imagined there were other mental realms that remain to be explored, and that science is still not fully understood.

The second step in getting yourself ready to enter an Akashic record is to engage with what the people of Eastern faiths are doing over many thousands of years. Meditation is a way to clear the mind, because it eliminates from the mind the energy sources, or forces that could steer your mind away from the sole achievement of an objective. Buddhists practice meditation when they wish to attain peace, because by meditative practice, they are able to take away the things in their environment that don't imply peace or reflect it, and then train the mind to believe in peace, be convinced of it, and strive towards it.

Meditation does not just remove away the things that can distract you from the mental task necessary to access your Akashic recording, but it is also a way to prepares your mind to take in information it might not be able to. As we've said before it is possible that you have unknowingly accessed Akashic records. It is possible that you were subjected to data from an etheric realm and could have become apathetic to it. Through meditation, you are able to teach your mind to take in all the information it can access information that extends back to the past as well as ahead into the future.

These two processes of meditation and desire are particularly important for those who haven't previously accessed the akashic record and may be skeptical about whether they are able to. You may be amazed by how significant desires are. The karmic idea that desires are the catalyst for actions is crucial to understand the intricate nature of Akashic records and accessing them. The karmic needs of humans aren't just recorded in the compendium known as called the Akashic records, however can be a tool can be used to gain access to these records.

In conjunction with the simple meditative practices like controlled breathing and clearing your mind and imagining an object in your mind (part of the transcendental practice) You may discover that you are able to access Akashic records isn't so far off as you thought it was.

Chapter 5: Exploring The Future And Altering The Past

If you believe in Akashic records, then you know that there exists a realm of existence where you've already had access to Akashic records since they have already been recorded, even though the is technically not happening in the present. It records are part of the recording of the actions and desires that are shared by everyone within this particular part that is the Universe. What you must do is take part in the nitty-gritty task of learning how to accomplish it, and thus fulfill the destiny that was already set for you.

You've been on an extensive journey in order to reach the present moment, which is the time in which you utilize all the knowledge you have gathered and direct it toward your desired goal. You are aware of the fundamental concept that is the Akashic record and know the realm of theosophic thought that it is a part of. You are familiar with the fundamental Brahmanic notions that underlie this concept: the notions of karma, samsara and the concept of dharma. These are the ideas that our deeds and our wishes result in an effect and that cause-and-effect relationships are found in the larger context of a common right way of life for people on earth.

Spiritually equipped with the wisdom of the akashic record, you can then to make your mind ready to be able to access the akashic records. First, you need clearing your mind of any thoughts or distractions that can steer you away from the absoluteness of your objective accessing the history of events from the past and future so that the present, past, and future seem to be in the same place. That way, you're in a position to alter everything around you, even fold space into itself by altering the time-based relationship of the universe.

When your mind is cleared, you can dive into the karmic realm to concentrate on what you want. The goal here could be to get access to the akashic records or something different. Maybe it's to meet somebody: someone who died some time ago or hasn't been born in the present. This is the dream which you can turn into actions, an action that already exists in the Akashic history of actions that took place to all humanity.

You've got your dream set in your mind, and you can visualize your goal, whatever it is. Your mind is clear and the object has taken up residence in your thoughts, becoming an area that you can dwell in. The room that you are in, the floor or the chair which you are sitting on the TV set and the bed all of it is not there. exist. The only thing that is there is the idea in your head that you are focused on. Over time, the idea develops into a reality that is its own. It's something that is present as like you and is its own place in the cosmic record.

When you return to this area and look around, you realize that your goal was completed. Maybe you talked to someone. Maybe you recognized faces of people, or you learned something. You entered an Akashic records and got to know the reality we once existed was a place of rules, of limitations as well as things that claim to exist, but in reality they don't and that the world is no more.

In this new world you have created through understanding that your previous world was a lie, you have done the following things:

* You have cleansed your mind of any distraction
* You have let go all tension that was holding your body as well as your mind.

* You've focused on your karmic wish and are aware that this will eventually lead to act

You've imagined the item you've long

* You've left the world to the side until it no longer exists.

* You have accomplished your dream and gained access to the Akashic record

Frequently asked questions

1. What do you think of these records? Akashic records?

Akashic records are the record of events, both past and in the future, within the cosmic space that Earth occupies. Akashic records exist for all the various regions of the universe, and as a person living on Earth you have the ability to get access to the Akashic record of your personal region in the world. Some people believe that the akashic records to be a part of a specific plane, an ethereal one which you are able to access. Some people view this akashic recording as an ancestral memory which you can gain access to as a descendant of the indestructible energy of the human experience on earth.

The term "akashic" records come from the Sanskrit word akasha meaning a vital force that is an ether that is, an atmospheric. It may be confusing for certain people to comprehend what it signifies, it is a very important concept. Think of this as a diary of events that occurred both in the past and the future that some individuals might have access to. The ability to access these records will provide you with an understanding of the events that occurred throughout time and maybe even the power to alter the events.

2. What is the Theosophy and what does it have to do with the akashic records?

Theosophy is a doctrine that was developed by the individual who brought the concept of akasha into the contemporary spirituality movement.

Theosophy is a belief in the universal brotherhood of all mankind but doesn't require followers to believe in a specific dogmatic doctrine. A lot of followers of this particular movement are a believer in the cosmological ideas that were developed by Blavatsky, Henry Olcott, Rudolf Steiner, and other early supporters of this particular form of spirituality.

Blavatsky herself was regarded as an occultist. She believed in some ideas that would be controversial in the present however they were not than they were in her time. Although Blavatsky believed in this tradition of universal brotherhood Blavatsky herself was not a believer in equality between races and many relied on her beliefs as the basis for policies regarding race in 1920s. Akashic records are one of the spiritual views that many of the followers of the movement adhere to although not all of the followers of the movement have the same beliefs.

3. Is it possible for anyone to have access Akashic records?

This is a fascinating question. If you adhere to the philosophies that was formulated by Blavatsky along with other theosophists those who are descendants of the ancestral races that resided in Atlantis, Lemuria, and other places ought to be capable of accessing Akashic records, as this is not just an aspect of memory of the ancestral past as well as an exclusive plane that must be available to people who are descended from these places. This does not mean that everyone today can have access to these records.

Theosophists from the beginning, as well as members of this group who adhere to the doctrine of this field will say that accessing the these akashic documents is a certain human potential. As a human is capable of becoming spiritually enlightened through Buddhist practices, Buddhist tradition, so be able to tap into these records. If they are aware of the significance of these records and how the human brain can be trained to recognize these records, most people could realize they are more accessible than they had previously believed.

4. Does science confirm or disprove the concept of Akshic records?

The official line of the theosophic community is that science hasn't given evidence of akashic records. However there are many brilliant minds in both the 20th and 21st centuries have been promoting ideas that appear to be in line with the concept that there is an Akashic record or hint at something that is that is similar. Stephen Hawking believed that science was on the verge of discovering the existence of alternative universes. This, while not exactly the same as those of Akashic record, could suggest some notions about time as it could be as simple as the scientific community believes. The possibility exists that we may be able to gain access to data from another universe, which isn't as different from the concept in the theosophy of the realm of the ethereal.

5. What is the difference between theosophy and anthroposophy?

Anthroposophy is a different spiritual school of thought that may be a little more specific in its beliefs than theosophy. The term "anthroposophy" refers to a philosophical system that believes that there is the spiritual world that humans can connect to through their minds. The school of thought is overlapping in a few ideas with that of theosophy at the very least, in relation to the specific beliefs that are embraced among prominent Theosophists. Anthroposophy has a long history of social activism, and the majority of its most famous members were involved in social movements, or other kinds of activism.

6. Do I need to be educated in order to access Akashic records?

The evidence suggests a clear connection between the concept of an Akashic recording and Buddhist notions of the universe. The first proponents of the akashic concept believed that Buddhist teachings hints that there was an Akashic record, as it understood the universe as one in which nothing is born from nothing and thus opening the way to a kind of record that existed on a particular plane which could be accessible. There is some speculation that people who are enlightened can access Akashic records however, there is no definitive affirmation that one needs to be spiritually enlightened in order to be able to access Akashic records.

7. Are people who are able to gain access Akashic records predict the future?

Some believe that there is a genuine clairvoyant, and others are able to anticipate the future access to Akashic records. Of course, they could not know they're doing it. Clairvoyants and other people who predict the future could be employing various methods, however they are generally believed to can read the energy fields of people and access information from both the past and present that are relevant to the person. This is similar to the akashic concept, the idea that there exists information on the time of events that people are in a position to access.

8. Are akasha and akashic recordings just the ideas of early theosophists such as Helena Blavatsky?

The terms akasha, akashic and akasha records might have been popularized by the early theosophists, but they're concepts and concepts which predate the movement by at minimum 2000 years. Akasha is one of the Sanskrit word in addition, its Sanskrit dialect is thought to be more than three thousand years old. Though inscriptions of this particular language can be less than 2000 years old, the texts which were composed in the language, and then preserved in daughter languages are older. Therefore Aksha, akashic and akasha records aren't new concepts or at least to people who are a believer in these concepts. They are rooted in practices that date back thousands of years old, which is more than the contemporary religious movement associated with anthroposophy or theosophy.

9. Do I have to meditate in order to gain access Akashic records?

Meditation is an essential element in gaining access to the Akashic records that form an essential part of theosophical tradition. The first Theosophists were adherents to Buddhist and Brahmanic tradition. These practices rely on meditation as a way to attain detachment and spiritual awakening. In actual fact having access to an Akashic record was considered as a feat only people who were spiritually enlightened could achieve.

In the end, most theosophists will be in agreement that you don't need to actively meditate to gain access to Akashic records, even though some people who can accomplish this could be in a state of meditation, but not being aware of it. While the majority of Americans might view meditation as doing chants, performing exercises, or specific mental and physical exercises, chanting could be just as easy as learning particular breathing strategies or clearing your thoughts in different ways. According to this book, certain people might have been born with the ability to gain access to Akashic records, without actually doing any meditation. Therefore, we can conclude that while practicing meditation could assist you in accessing Akashic records, but it is not the only requirement for learning this skill.

10. Do I have to believe in atheism while adhere to and practice access to akashic records?

The idea that the Akashic record does not mean the belief in a specific system. The concept of akashic records stems from concepts that are derived directly from traditions like Buddhism and Hinduisms which are belief systems which the practitioners believed in a variety of gods. Despite these roots they simply state that there is a collective data as a result of the events of every human being (and other animals according to what you believe) that are being documented.

Traditions of atheism go back to thousands of years ago and atheists are found in the context of Brahmanic or Buddhist India. In other words, the ancient minds could reconcile their beliefs regarding the concept of karma as well as the cyclical nature life in the universe and many other ideas with their own belief in the existence of God. While some themes are reflected in Akashic documents, the specific belief in God isn't among them. Theosophists typically have a variety of beliefs in religion, because theosophy, like the belief systems of Asia tends to be more of a religious belief as opposed to it is a religion.

11. How can I tell what a subjective experience is an intuitive feeling or "sixth sense" instead of actually using or accessing the Akashic record?

Some theosophists claim that it is necessary to have a person who is skilled within spirituality or the "occult" to be able to discern what is a sensation that could be a result of an accident or a manifestation of intuition that is triggered by having access to an Akashic record. Anyone who has studied spirituality is likely to have an understanding of where a certain source of knowledge came from. This is different from people who are not as experienced and may just have a vague feeling but do not know the source.

What we do we try to accomplish within this publication is to give readers an understanding of how you can train your mind to read documents and thus be more certain that the information you are receiving comes from one source and not from another. It's not an easy task. The clairvoyant might not know exactly the source of their information however, some, such as those who are studying the fields of cosmology and spirituality, might know that they're accessing the record, rather than having a sense of the person they are observing.

Chapter 6: Soul Purpose

The purpose of your soul is the reason that you're in this world right now. The thing you're searching for is likely to be connected to the purpose for your spirit. It's an aspect of your life which inspires and pushes you ahead. If you understand what your soul's mission is then you'll be content with your life.

Humans are quite complex. We're a bit complicated "mission" as humans is to feed, reproduce and spread. But every one person has a more important, personal mission. Find the next treatment for a rare illness and establishing an animal sanctuary or promoting the equality of race could be the soul's mission. You Soul mission is exclusive to you and you're the only one who can fulfill it.

It is difficult to connect with the Soul's mission often since we're not connected to our Soul's purpose at all! That is, we've created a state called Soul Loss. We've lost

75

contact with our Souls as a result of the trauma of early indoctrination the self-destructing effects of abuse, self-neglect and toxic core beliefs, and the lack of an education that is Soul-centered.

Connection with other people and the feeling of sacredness and connection the God we once worshipped are now replaced by mechanical or materialistic possession.

I'm not saying that the sciences and logic are crucial. But, we end up losing our Souls when we put too heavily in" the "yang," or the masculine-driven concepts of development, success and victory.

In order to regain our Souls, we have to perform Soul Retrieval. We need to find the divine feminine, or yin inside us (a female-free power).

Soul Retrieval is a process that can be achieved by a variety of methods:

Meditation and visualization trips

Utilizing inner archetypes to aid in the process of constructing tools

Experimenting various levels of consciousness

Exercises to help self-compassion, and love for yourself.

Develop your inner child and shadow.

How can we tell when we've been able to recover our Soul? This is a wonderful idea, and my initial conclusion is that you'll feel it immediately.

In terms of feeling, you'll be more energetic, rejuvenated and energized. You'll feel more energetic, vibrant as well as inspired. You may even feel "reborn."

The characteristics to cultivate in order to find the soul's motivation

Honesty is the key to being truthful with your self.

Affirmation of Gratitude - Be conscious of the things in your life that you are thankful. This helps you open your soul, and can be an entry point into your soul.

Open to learning and ready to accept them into your life.

Believe in your intuition and discovers.

Regularly practicing your spirituality can help you to develop or enhance these abilities.

How to Live and Find Your Soul's purpose

The process will become simpler to find your Soul's purpose after you've regained accessibility to this. However, it won't be simple! Your Soul is not linear: it predates and surpasses your mind, in each aspect. Here are two suggestions to aid you in your mystical journey to self-actualization, self-realization and self-realization

1. Make sure to capture those happy Wisps in the air

There have been those bizarre and enchanting encounters that leave us in admiration, amazement admiration, fascination, and even inspiration. Many people don't pay attention to them and continue to go about their daily lives while claiming they're "imagining" things or being in a mood of awe! The phantom light of happiness must be taken seriously. They are crucial.

Maybe it was a reminiscence music track, a butterfly flying through the air, or perhaps a raindrop falling down the window, which created the most magical moment of pure happiness for you. Do not let that tiny bit of happiness disappear into thin air. Take note! Take an instant. Better yet, keep a notebook and record the significance it had to you.

These odd occurrences often carry powerful messages. Think about the following scenario that I was feeling down the one day when I was feeling overwhelmed and depressed. When I looked out the window, admiring the lush green shrubs that swayed in the breeze my spirit lifted. Like this plant was battling me to build me up. Plants cannot develop deep roots unless it's been weathered.

2. Stillness, silence and the solitude

The ego, a fake mask to hide the soul, creates lots of chaos disturbance, noise, and confusion throughout our lives. The ego is necessary to function however it has a habit of hindering our most cherished desires and needs.

To understand the purpose of your Soul To discover your Soul's purpose, you must break away from your self-centeredness. It is also important to stay away from the egos of other people (because they can reinforce your personal ego). Therefore, it is natural to seek solitude. is the best approach to entering the realm of the soul's mysteries.

If you're lucky enough to have the option of having a break or getting away from the stresses of your daily life, head to a place that is wild. To escape from the bustle and noise of suburban or city life, be surrounded by the roars of wolves, the chirps of birds and the gentle rustle of the tree branches.

Literature's greatest works (such like Henry David Thoreau's Walden and May Sarton's Journal of a Solitude) were written in silence. The first time ever, being in solitude allows the Soul's voice to be heard. You'll need a diary or notebook take one with you!

Self-Realization

You're probably trying to balance an hour-long work week as well as a family and expenses. You've gotten tired of those demands put on you through the decades. You're not at ease with your personal life. In reality, you're under the perception that your circumstances have control over you.

What if there were an option to gain control of your life and create positive changes? It's possible through being aware. You've heard of this idea but you're not sure what it is, but it could be beneficial to you. How often do you find yourself lost, distracted by your thoughts, or get overwhelmed by anxiety and fear?

Being present is more difficult than ever before due to our technological advancements of today. People are often glued to their laptops or smartphones in complete disbelief that the people in their vicinity are competing at their attention. Most people do not spend a lot of time in their current situation. They are injured or are unable to let go of the past, or are preoccupied with their future plans.

Here are a few of the Amazing Benefits of Self-Awareness:

The ability to track your emotions is a must. apply what you learned about your feelings throughout the conversation to manage worry, fear and tension. Self-realizations can help teach you to release your burdensome emotions and accept positive ones.

Focus and concentration improvement Focus and concentration improvement:

Self-realization, guided your personal goals and values helps you find and eliminate distractions. When you get rid of persons or events to keep your attention on the most important things and will allow you to realize all the potential of your abilities.

Self-esteem, confidence and confidence all rise and you're free from the dreadful feeling of self-worth, anxiety and fears through letting you know that they don't really define you.

Self-acceptance and acceptance by others: You are able to be more genuine and share your feelings more clearly. Instead of trying to impress people and impress them, you could build deeper connections with them and spend more time with them.

People who do not have a solid sense of their own self are easily influenced to follow the advice of others to do. Self-awareness offers a place of refuge.

Methods to Start the Process

1. Start practicing regular meditation: Meditation is an excellent method of achieving self-realization.

Find the chair that is appropriate to your requirements.

Begin by making sure your eyes are open and your eyes focusing softly.

Inhale deeply through your nose, and then out of your mouth for approximately 1 minute.

Relax your eyes and close them after taking a couple of deep breaths. Exhale.

Bring your breathing back to normal.

Pause for a moment and savor the fact that there is nothing to do, no where to be, or no one to look up.

Imagine the strain on the seat beneath you as you sit with your feet on the ground and your hands and arms reclining on your legs.

Bring your attention back to your breath.

Do not try to control your thoughts while you sit watching your breath , and the changing sensations within your body. Let them go in and out at any time they wish.

When you realize that your mind is wandering, the only thing you need to do is gently return it to your breathing.

Begin to pay attention to the feeling of being attuned to your surroundings and your surrounding environment, and then you can open your eyes slowly as you're at the right moment.

Yoga is another excellent way to attain self-realization that requires some strength. Although yoga has become an exercise that is well-known within Western society, the idea behind it was to use it as an intentional practice to attain the higher level of consciousness that is associated with self-realization.

2. Take time each day to be aware of your self. 40% of the things you do throughout the day do not require an active choice. It's more about habits over any other thing. There's probably some bad habits in

your numerous. If you can keep the track of your routines There is a simple way to alter a bad behaviour into something that is better. Make changes to your environment to make changing your behavior simpler.

Instead of finding time to complete something, the aim is to alter the routine that you follow daily. Imagine that you start your day by making coffee before sitting down at the tables for 20 mins to read your newspaper. Why not take the 20 minutes in meditation rather than watching news that can be packed with disturbing information?

Soul Transcendence

The realisation of your being a soul connected to God is referred to as soul transcendence. If our thoughts and our presence are in sync with our awareness of the soul as well as God, we live an existence of soul transcendence.

In this world, our consciousness is often condensed into a physical shape. It's not attracted by other things. There's more that is not visible to our eyes, and it's not heard by the ears of our own; our skin doesn't detect it. Although our senses are oblivious to it, that aspect of us which is an extension to a higher consciousness recognizes that there's more to life than our physical body.

It is your responsibility to discover certain aspects of your own self, and you accomplish it in different ways. But, all of us follow one fundamental rule That is: You're here to find out who you really are, discover and enter that Soul world, and be in the co-creative awareness of God.

In times of desperation, your need for peace and happiness could be the trigger that energizes you spiritually since the peace you desire is peace of your soul.

You are already the person you want to be. You've already reached the luminosity.

You're already the most perfect perfection within your Soul.

"The Soul" (who is you) is an extremely small, integrated energy unit which is so large that it encompasses the entire universe, including all the universes. It's a representation for everything that exists and is condensed into one energy unit. There is nothing in the galaxies you're not an integral part of due to the energy of the Soul. "I are" is a term used to describe "soul." It is the most advanced level of consciousness that is available at a physical level. It is the soul's intelligence. it is able to comprehend.

The Soul's goal or purpose for existence is to become aware of its divinity by being able to experience everything that is possible on every level. And the Soul that's gone through all of it has become part of God. The Soul recognizes that it's always been all of these things but was always what it is: a Soul, an integral element of God.

The goal of your Soul's journey is to recover consciousness and a sense of oneness with God. This path is referred to by The Soul Transcendence Path.

There is a path to Rejoin God.

Soul Transcendence means to experience and be present with God and to be aware of it. When we speak of Soul Transcendence, it is about awakening the soul and activating it to be as pure Spirit. The way toward Soul Transcendence is simple. There is no reason for you to do anything extra. Be aware of everything going on around as well as within you, then, follow the heart of love.

If you are able to transcend these dangerous levels and look through the Soul, you are able to rise up in consciousness and know the location of your home and the route that will lead you to get there. You travel through your

Sound Current, the highest energy force, also known as the Holy Spirit God's unspoken Voice the Spirit's unstruck Melodies. Through the absence of form you are guided by your Sound Current back to God's heart. This"Sound" Current is the acoustic energy flowing from God across all dimensions. This is the same spiritual force that allows one to return to the core of God.

The process establishes a connection with The Sound Current, which we continue to follow to God throughout all realms. With the help of Soul Transcendence, also known as the Mystical Traveler Consciousness and Soul Transcendence students are engulfed to the sound Current that is an audible flow of energy emanating from the center of God.

The Function of Ascension
Spiritual Ascension

Spiritual ascension is often a source of anxiety since it requires us to think about what we're about and what's the reason for our existence. Knowing the answer on these queries will help you feel alive. Spiritual ascension can be initiated by any event that is from the smallest to the most profound event.

Signs and signs of spiritual ascension

Here are some indicators that you're experiencing or close to experiencing an ascension spiritual experience:

1. You feel a sense of disconnection or separation at first, the spiritual ascension process can be confusing and overwhelming.

2. You've changed your mind Spiritual ascension is likely to make you reconsider or accept major changes to your spiritual convictions.

3. Your dreams have become more apparent Spiritual ascensions can enrich your life in the present however, it could

help you live your dream life to the fullest extent.

4. You're experiencing more synchronicities as well as the feeling of deja familiarity: If you're experiencing amazing synchronicities, then you're on the right path.

5. The dynamics of your relationships change: Spiritual awakenings are life-changing experiences and those you are living with may not be aware of this.

6. It's been apparent that spirituality is getting more crucial in your daily life: Finding meaning and satisfaction in your spiritual life will surely be one of your most important goals.

7. You've got a more powerful intuition The fact is that you've always had an intuition however since you've woken up, you're able to tap into it since you're more in touch with your own.

8. You can spot deceit and manipulation. Alongside your increased awareness, you

are able to spot any dishonesty or exploitative behavior when someone is attempting to fool you.

9. Everyone is on their own path things like winning arguments or convincing people to support your position aren't as crucial as they were in the past.

10. You're looking to help others. As you discover that all living creatures are equal and worthy You will be inspired to help animals, people or the planet. To make your life feel worthwhile, you need to have an issue that you are able to unite behind.

11. Your teachers have noticed that during ascension ceremony, your spiritual masters might "come to you with perfect timing to aid you. They could be a friendly customer in the store or an unexpected acquaintance or even a spiritual leader.

12. There is a feeling of loneliness. Spiritual ascension can be challenging. There is a chance to awaken to an

alternate side, this may be lonely --
especially in the case that your family and
friends don't share the same beliefs with
you.

13. A deeper connection: You'll sense a
connection to all things from animals to
plants to the whole world and it could be
quite emotional.

14. The senses are now more alert during
spiritual ascension. you'll often feel more
alert when you tune into the present.
Physical and emotional as well as
energetic sensitiveness are all instances of
this.

15. There may be an increase in body
sensations. Your increased awareness and
perception could be coupled with other
physiological reactions. Sleep Apnea is a
frequent situation.

16. You might experience physical signs
spiritual ascension may cause a variety of
physical symptoms which indicate a health
concern.

17. Your routine and routines have abruptly changed as your spiritual life changes, your everyday life, including the practices and rituals will begin to shift.

18. The world is now seen differently spiritual ascension can be a bit tangled and can cause you to see your self as a part of a larger world.

19. Empathy: You'll develop more empathy for the pain of other people; you will feel more inclined to help.

20. You've revived the passion you had for something. Now you've made an " ascendance " to the realm of your own existence it's more likely that you'll keep your interest in the things you love even in times of difficulty.

The Ascension process and the phases of ascension

True ascension typically is a slow process, and the process is split into multiple phases, in the following order:

1. The awakening: In this phase you eliminate certain areas of your life in order to let in newand more fulfilling experiences. There's a sense that something isn't quite right however you're not certain which one it is.

2. The dark night: It's one of the most challenging times, one of the most challenging. This is the time that your soul is refining it's self in various ways, and removing the self-image so that you can create a major change.

3. The sponge: You're now ready to live in your brand new way of life. You continue to experiment to discover what is a good fit for your soul. Then you begin to explore and look into other things like thoughts as well as relationships and so on.

4. Satoru in this phase you start to recognize and accept your strengths.

5. The soul's sessions the fifth stage. This can take a long time to finish. The physical structure is put that you have put in place

to allow your spirit to blossom. It may require some trials and errors and many different options. In this period your spirit is thriving and healing.

6. The surrender is the last step of the process of awakening, and it is the process of letting go any remaining ego-based patterns and beliefs or character traits that hinder you from experiencing your true self.

7. Public awareness and service Your consciousness is now aware of your divinity and you're in a state of clarity which can bring you a huge amount of happiness and satisfaction.

Spiritual Ascension , and the Akashic Record

The word Akashic originates from the primordial elements in Ayurveda which is an eastern science. These five components that constitute nature's elements include air (Vayu) and water (jala) (jala), as well as ether (akash) and fire (agni) and the earth (bhumi). Because it was the very first element to be created, ether, also known as Akash is considered to be the most important element in Vedic Cosmology. It shouldn't be considered to be the fifth element since it acts as the base of the four other elements. Akash is a space in where energy and sound freely move It is believed to be the place where everything converges and connects. According to the yoga tradition that is based on sound and vibration, they are crucial because thoughts and intentions thoughts are the basis of reality. This essential element is the key to ascending into the Fifth Dimension and beyond by getting access to the Akashic recordings.

Akashic records are believed to be a record for the past, the present and the future, which includes all parallel universes, multiverses and omniverse as well as all the higher dimensions of infinite and beyond. The Akashic records symbolize God's collective consciousness which contains the electromagnetic frequencies of all ideas in every universe that has existed since the beginning of the universe.

It also takes into consideration the possibility of future results. Since our minds need linear understanding, we refer to Akashic recordings to be "records" as well as "a collection" filled with information. Akashic recordings however are multi-dimensional.

How can you access the Akshic records?

The purpose of having access to the records is to boost the rate of your vibration to reach an increased level of understanding. To begin, you need to be convinced that it exists and have access to relevant records. To be able to access the Akashic records which are believed to be the realm within the Fifth Dimension and beyond, you must leave the limitations and thinking of the third dimension. To put it in another way before you can be able to tune into what you are seeking it is necessary to develop your brain to understand the notion.

When you are able to access your insights or intuition it is a sign that you have access to an Akashic record. The Akashic records don't exist physically anywhere, but they're an experience, rather than an idea. exercises like meditation or breathing can aid in raising your frequency.

It is the Akashic And Chakra Records

Chakra-energy work is a different method to gain access to your Akashic information. The process involves tuning into your chakras and allow your higher-level perspective to move through your body as an audio channel through every chakra, matching your chakras' vibrations to the information that you want to access.

This "information" comes from your Akashic records is transmitted directly from the higher Self and enters your body through your Crown Chakra, disseminated and stored in the chakras. It is possible that your higher self would like to grant you confidence in yourself and self-confidence. This information will be delivered to you via The Solar Plexus Chakra, which is the source of your power. The Sacral Chakra will be receiving information regarding one's self-worth as well as interpersonal connection. In our Earthly journey the root chakra that anchors us Root Chakra will receive everything that is related to security and safety. The process will continue until you've obtained the essential tools for living your life and achieving the purpose of your soul.

Your knowledge, wisdom and the information you have gained from previous lives and experiences and your current life are stored in our minds. The frequency and complexity of the form grow as you progress from a lower to higher level. This sacred space holds all the information that needs to be kept or accessible when needed. Anyone can gain access to all the knowledge that is stored in the Akashic records of the body and the soul.

Cosmology - The Planes of Existence
Levels Of Existence
Mann (mind) and buddhi (intellect) Chitta (memory) and ahankaara are all parts of the same conscious (ego).
Mind
How do you concentrate your attention and listen to them even if your thoughts are somewhere else? You're hearing through your mind and this is a faculties inside you. You can choose to taking a moment of silence, eyes closed or wide. Remove your mind from all senses, and only then can you begin to meditate.
Tension and stress are the primary causes for negative thoughts. If you've been

sleeping in two consecutive days, the smallest discomforts can cause irritation. But things will be different when you've had an enjoyable night's sleep.

When you regularly practice meditation the mind gets more alert, active and perceptive.

Intellect

When you listen, you're either being in agreement or disagreement. Pay attention to whether you're using 'yes' or 'no.' The mind is what allows us to express "yes" as well as "no."

Life can be difficult to comprehend. There's no one-size-fits-all solution. If you believe you're sincere and moral but you become stiff in the midst of your body without realizing it. If you are pointing fingers at other people, you create an intolerant attitude. If you are willing to accept your weaknesses then you can allow for the flaws of other people.

More than your faults or bad traits can harm your health. Even your strengths could make you rigid, harsh, and angry. In the end, you need to shed both your positive and negative attributes.

Memory

Your memories may make you sad or inspire you. Meditation can assist you in getting rid of painful memories. Introspection can aid you in making the necessary shift and help you to regain the true you.

Your ego as well as your emotions

Check your own psychological and mental patterns; they are based on patterns. There is also the mental beat. The internal and external rhythms have to be in harmony, and that is the essence of spirituality.

Check yourself thoroughly. Are you in the same boat with you? Yesterday you had a thought and you might have a different idea today. You had different thoughts five years ago that could be similar to the ones you are currently thinking about. Why should it be different from others when you aren't in agreement with you? Someone who you do not agree with is simply a copy of your previous or new self.

Maintaining interpersonal relationships requires the following steps:

A relation with oneself. This is described as being honest.

Being casual gives greater room for errors. This helps maintain the integrity of a strong interpersonal connection.

Every day is to be treated as if it were. It's normal to be sad or angry when you feel it; it's normal. Relax and let the things happen according to their own schedule.

The Cycle Of Karma

Karma is the result of your choices in the present and in previous lives.

Karmic cycles are an arrangement that is designed for you to learn a lesson. Souls accumulate karmic debts during each life, and must be returned in the following life. The observation of patterns that are repeated throughout your life will assist you in determining what obligations you have to pay.

Have you ever had the joy of a moment, only to be and then a bout of luck? Have you ever had an ephemeral moment of happiness after a time of solitude? Have you ever told your self, "I am the luckiest person on earth," after which you wondered, "Why on Earth does it happen to me every time?" For sure, you aren't the only one. This happens to everyone at the time of their lives because everything revolves around a circle of karmic karma. The law of karma operates in cycles.

Karma originates of the Sanskrit language, which means "activity.' In Hindu mythology it has a lengthy and fascinating time. However, it did become popular throughout Jainism, Buddhism, and various other religions throughout the years.

A lot of people are afraid by the concept of "karma." Inspiring phrases like 'May Karma never be able to find you' or "Karma will take charge of you' can cause people to believe that the Universe is treating them unfairly. They'll eventually be faced with what they call the "wrath of Karma." But the reality is far from this false assumption.

Karma isn't just only a single instance of revenge or wrath neither is it an individual moment of pleasure or death. It's that's everything there's to know about it. Each other element of the universe works in the same way. It describes how each bit of energy you use is returned to you whether it is instantaneously or over a period of time.

The physical reality of existence

Physical plane is the tangible physical reality that exists in both temporal and spatial scales, energy, as well as matter in metaphysics of emanations. It is the smallest or most dense of a sequence of existence (hyperplanes which are thought to be nestled).

The mental plane's existence

Mental plane also known as the realm of thought is the macrocosmic or universal realm of reality that is made up of thoughts or mind-stuff. It is found that is found in the Hermeticism movement, Theosophy, Rosicrucianism, Aurobindonianism as well as New Age philosophy. It is just one of the many variations in an array of levels. The mental plane acts to act as an intermediate between higher spiritual realms of the sky and the lower astral plane below.

Mastering Plans

Existence plans

The universe is filled with worlds, and there are a myriad of diverse worlds that GMs use to play their games, confined in the rather ordinary realm of the material Plane as well as the angels' and devils lairs and the domains of gods.

The Material Plane

In the chaotic world of human life and everyday substances The Material Plane is the place where all different worlds meet. It is the Material Plane contains all fantasy gaming realmsand serves as the basis for defining the other universes.

Planes in Transit

The Transitive Planes include The Ethereal Plane as well as the Astral Plane They are the conduits between planes that have been compared to the vast ocean. A few magical effects can be seen beyond the Material Plane to the Ethereal Border. Ethereal.

Toroidal Field

Surrender

The universe was born from the endless possibilities of the universe's pure presence. As you're constantly wondering what it was that created it the simple logic says it didn't come from any 'creative being.' While creative people have created aspects of the universe since they were born (for example, our civilisation) however, they haven't created the basis of existence itself. It's pure consciousness from the foundation of all things.

Pure consciousness refers to the consciousness that emerged from the beginning in the form of waves of relativity with an infinity of time, it is the potential to occur in an infinite amount of time. According to quantum scientists the Big Bang was preceded by ripples of space.' The waves propagated outwards in the form of a chain reaction.

The erupting of the singularity was balanced by an equally opposite flow outwards. The universe breathed the first huge exhalation that was swiftly followed by an inhalation that was

110

counterbalanced. The individual consciousness was consolidated into the many shapes we see in the present due to the pull back towards unity.

It's interesting to think about the scientific basis behind it, however, it's much better to discover the truth through deep contemplation in your own return to your root. It is when you begin to recognize your own creative potential which gave the world. Eureka. You've returned to the pleasures of life!

Meditational Exercises

In your own time you are able to engage in a range of meditation techniques. You may also participate in the activities as part of an organization. The term "contemplative" can be described as any act that can help relax the mind in order to be able to observe the world in silence through.

Meditations can take a variety of types, and include, but not only:

Practice diaphragmatic breathing

Methods to relax

Imagery directed and visual

Meditation to focus your attention

Mindfulness for Focused and Directed

Progressive Relaxation (PRM) can be described as a kind of meditation that combines the body in search of meditation.

Mindfulness-based training

Breath Awareness Mindfulness

Transcendental Meditation (TM) is a form of meditation which focuses in Zen meditation.

Meditation and yoga

A focused practice can assist you to to become better at paying focus. It's a technique of meditation in which you set your focus on a single thing. It is a way to focus your attention only on the object and completely forgetting all other distractions.

Increased State of Awareness

The state of awareness is the level which is the awareness that something is taking place. Humans are able to experience either increased or diminished levels of awareness and the latter is responsible for subconscious and reflexive actions.

To increase their level of consciousness, an individual is attentive and pays focus on specific aspects they may be focusing on or occurring in their surroundings. For instance the challenge of solving the Rubik's Cube, deciding which clothes to wear or taking notes during the course.

There can still be distractions , even while engaging in these activities This is the reason the reason why you're in a state of awareness. In a state of increased awareness your mind is cleared free of any clutter (distractions). The attention is laser-focused on detail followed by an in-depth review of all actions happening in the vicinity.

Anyone who can achieve this level will have more ability to control their thinking. This can lead to the state of mindfulness. A state of mind (a state of increased awareness) can be realized when someone is fully conscious of the thoughts that are in their mind. It's about making the effort of examining the thoughts of one's mind, for instance when one considers why they behaved in a specific way, just a few seconds after the answer was made.

One way to achieve this state of awareness is to meditate that helps you focus on the present moment with the mind at peace.

Get rid of the clutter in your Head

The mental or head clutter could be caused by a variety of things including getting up over opinions of other people and past mistakes (and keeping the past mistakes) or trying to keep everything under control, even when there are things that are beyond control.

One can only attain greater awareness by having an uncluttered mind. Additionally, a mind that is cluttered can only lower one's daily productivity. Therefore, it is a need to rid your mind of any clutter to live a better and more enjoyable life.

Here are six methods to clear the head:

1. Don't try to be all things to everyone, because it's impossible regardless of how you try.

2. Be aware of things that are beyond the control of you and allow them to them go. them.

3. Let go of the past , and embrace the present. This means, you should cherish every moment of your life and especially with the people you cherish.

4. Organise your day by making to-do lists of the tasks that must be completed every day. Focus on a few most important tasks. Other tasks, particularly repetitive are best transferred or automated.

5. Limit your time using screens. No matter if they're mobile phones laptops, tablets, TVs or other devices the devices can generate a lot of head clutter, and restricting the time spent on them will help you reduce clutter considerably.

6. Do a meditation practice as a everyday routine. This can help you clear your head allow you to attain mindfulness, and increase your ability to focus.

Meditation: Get rid of the clutter Within Your Head

Meditation is an extremely effective method to unclutter your mind. It offers many advantages that it can be a wonderful relaxation tool and can generally improve your lifestyle. Apart from being a powerful method to improve stress resistance it also has a spiritual value because it provides inner peace. To live peace and tranquility it is necessary to be able to master this art.

There are a variety of methods of meditation, and mindfulness meditation is one of the most popular methods to increase awareness. Here are the steps to Practice Mindful Meditation:

1. Find a quiet spot Be away from any disturbance or noise

2. Be patient: There's no time limit set for meditation. The length of time one is able to meditate is contingent upon various factors like the person's age, determination or experience as a meditation therapist and many more. For people who are just beginning, it is recommended to start with a shorter time of 5 to 10 minutes as a starting point.

3. Select a position that is suitable If you assume that any position is perfect for meditation. It doesn't matter if you're lying down or sitting on your knees, a chair, crisscrossing, whatever. Make sure your body is comfortable so that you're

able to stay steady in the position you're in.

4. Watch your breathing pattern Pay attention to your breathing patterns closely while you breathe in and exhale.

5. Refocus quickly Attention spans are typically very short and are difficult to keep. You'll probably lose focus on how your body moves. If you notice this, you should quickly pay focus to your breathing rhythm.

6. Don't be a victim of being lost: Sure your mind may wander at some point, but don't let you to lose yourself in your thoughts or feel harsh on yourself for allowing it occur. You can regain your focus after you've spotted the issue.

7. Begin with a calm consciousness: When the moment is over and you're ready to finish your meditation, take the focus back on your present surroundings with a gentle touch. Take your eyes off (if the eyes were shut) and gaze around and

become conscious of your surroundings by paying attention to your feelings, the sensation in your own body your sounds as well as your thoughts, and anything else that is happening in your immediate surroundings. Thank them for everything.

Make sure you follow these steps as gently as you can, as you watch your consciousness rise significantly.

Initiating and Aligning Your Chakras

Based on Buddhism, Kabbalah, and Hinduism the chakras are energy pools that are located in our bodies , which are linked with the nerve system, specific organs, and regulate our psychological state. In general there are seven primary chakra points throughout the body. Working on and aligning them can enable a person to experience physical, emotional and spiritual peace.

Each chakra points controls specific aspects of one's life and is colored differently. They are located at the base chakra, or the root chakra and move to that of the crown chakra. Here are the seven primary chakras, along with their color depiction and what they represent:

1. The Root Chakra (Muladhara) is red and is located near the anus. It is a symbol of mental awareness and instinct and the ability to survive.

2. It is the Sacral Chakra (Svadhisthana) is located in the genital area just below the belly button. It is a symbol of creative quotient, emotional quotient and sexuality.

3. The Solar chakra plexus (Manipura) has a yellow color. it is located in the stomach region . It regulates wisdom, life, and character.

4. The Heart Chakra (Anahata) is green and can be found at the center of the chest. It represents compassion love, healing, and love.

5. The Throat Chakra (Vishuddha) is blue and located within the throat. It

symbolizes inspiration as well as spoken communication.

6. The Third Eye Chakra (Ajna) is a deep blue that is located in the forehead, in between the eyes. It symbolizes determination, gut instinct and imagination.

7. The Crown Chakra (Sahasrara) is purple and is located on the top of the head. It represents the spiritual, purposeful and consciousness.

After all seven chakra points are activated there will be a balance and they're able to be activated by meditation.

Meditation: Align and Activate Chakras

Take these actions to align and activate your chakras by meditative:

1. Recognize every chakra place

2. Find a peaceful spot to relax and meditate.

3. Relax and take deep breaths.

4. Focus on each chakra, moving from the beginning to the

5. Spend time at each chakra, reinvigorating them.

6. See the alignment and alignment for each chakra by rotating them clockwise

7. Then bring the meditation to an end, and gradually return to your daily activities and daily life.

Chapter 7: Coherence, And The New Human

This brand new human idea examines the infinite possibilities for humans to develop. This includes interactions with other (non-human) creatures with higher levels of intelligence, and acknowledging that there is genetic connections between all living things. Through the experiences of hundreds of people around the globe who have encountered these non-human or alien life forms, we can see that they played an important part in the development of humankind to a greater level of consciousness.

This is a way to achieve coherence, which is a state in which everything is rational, and all thoughts, theories or events as well as the internal workings of consciousness of all living forms are logically arranged as a whole plan of the universe.

Anyone can attain coherence however it begins with understanding your personal state.

Your Nature State

The majority of people consider struggle, the feeling of suffering, anger, anxiety, and fear as normal and natural however, these emotions are reactions, not essential or normal characters. We show these emotions only when confronted with external circumstances and when we are feeling at risk.

Our state of being is one of love and serene, with an awareness of calm and peace. We respond to external disruptions in our equilibrium state when it is disturbed. If we're free from the events that happen in the life, we're by nature, tranquil blessed and content beings.

Brain Waves

Brain waves are created through the interplay with millions of nerve cells among themselves, which results in the synchronization of electrical impulses. These waves are the basis for all actions, thoughts and feelings and are further subdivided into moderate, fast as well as slow ones.

Brainwaves are a great analogy to brainwaves. They is musical notes, in which the low frequency waves have similarities to the beat of a drum , which can penetrate deeply, and waves with higher frequencies are like an instrument with soft high pitch.

The activities we engage in during the day determine which brainwaves we show. Brainwaves are low when we are tired or dull, as well as high brainwaves when we are hyperactive. The unit of measurement used for the speed of brain waves is Hertz which is the amount of cycles per second.

A fast-moving wave signifies that the brain is active, stimulated and in a high alertness state. Fast waves are also known as Gamma (35 Hz and higher) as well as beta waves (12 up to 35 Hz) which are the most rapid. They are low in amplitude. People who show these waves usually engages in tasks such as decision-making and problem-solving.

A moderate wave can be observed when one is calm and in a state of mind, such as in meditation or when completing an assignment. These comprise Alpha wave (8 -12 Hz). They are more powerful than gamma and beta, which indicate a lack of arousal.

Slow waves are referred to as Theta (8 4-Hz) or Delta waves (0.5 to 4 Hz) They are the most powerful and the lowest frequencies. Humans display these waves during moments of deep relaxation like when they sleep. In reality, one can feel this way during the course of a job but the task is carried out in an autopilot mode, which allows the individual to withdraw from the task.

Ascending from Beta Brain Waves

It is important to seek ascending from one brainwave to another. This is why, even though it's the fastest wave beta brain waves could create stress if the person is exposed to them, and this can affect our health.

Ascension Into Gamma

Gamma waves are among the fastest of all waves. those who exhibit this type of wave are experiencing a higher state of consciousness. In this state the brain's neurons are connected at the same time.

People with this kind of brain activity can remember events quickly and clearly, and can be awoken by with a heightened sense of kindness and love. These individuals are on the highest level of their cognitive performance and have high levels of intelligence and are more self-controlled.

In general, you'll see martial arts masters as well as spiritualists and Buddhists who exhibit gamma brainwaves. However, one doesn't need to be one of them to function at this degree. Anyone can be able to ascend into the gamma brainwaves by using any of the following:

1. Socializing with friends who have already reached Gamma.

2. Utilizing brainwave entrainments to allow people to synchronize with the brainwave frequency that they prefer.

3. It is important to eat more plant-based meals with high vibrational and nutritional value.

Average Human

Humanity hasn't reached coherence, and is still functioning at the same level in the world. The average human isn't in the state of being an entirely new human.

Syntropy

Syntropy is the state in which an individual feels totally connected to others psychologically.

Akashic Records

The Akashic record opens the way into a new dimension of your life that you may not have known about. It's a dimension which is a part "Consciousness." The understanding of the akashic recording will provide you with an thorough understanding of the journey of your life as well as your soul's total knowing. It allows you to live an enlightened and meaningful life in which you are able to learn more about your previous lives and the ways in which your life are leading you to.

Your soul doesn't have no any purpose. The universe is guiding you to a place that you need to discover to lead a more fulfilled and more fulfilling life, and to reach an enlightened version of yourself. You're most powerful in the highest point in your spiritual journey. The akashic records will light your path to understanding mysteries of the universe .

It will also aid you find a meaning in your life.

What are the records of the akashic?

There are many different ways to define the akashic archives in different ways, but in the end they're believed as a record of all living things' thoughts and actions and speech, as well as emotion and emotion, alive or dead and good or bad and at all times of existence; past, present and the future. The akashic files record the journey of the soul through all of its life, linking the present self to its past lives as well as the future self. There is no punishment or judgments in its records.

Akashic Records, also referred to as the hall of records is derived via the Indian word Akasha. Akasha is the first of the major elements. The Akasha is where the creation process is brought together in fire, air water, earth, and air and is the source of the beginning of matter. The Akasha was there before everything other, and it is the basis of everything that returns to.

The akashic records as well as our universe This universe forms an essential component of the Akashic record. The person you are marks by the universe. What is to come or what is happening are all recorded into the universe. The body is awash with energy through a medium referred to by the name of "Line in the." The energy that flows through it comes from the most heavenly realms of the universe and is also where our akashic recording is found. The constant messages and messages are received by these lines, then are thought to be an inner understanding which is a sense of self-perception that will guide you on your entire journey. This line connects your soul to the world of your akashic records, giving you an access point to all of the world, and continuously transmitting messages to assist you in understanding the reason you're in this planet and why you've been given to be here for.

Healing within the Akashic records

By activating your inner line, it gives you the ability to receive assistance along with guidance from higher-self about what you can do to recover or develop your soul in a difficult or even impossible circumstance. Help your line to activate its universal activation and earth point. Then, become your true self to change your life. Connect to your akashic record and take note of the messages that will help you through your healing process.

If you're struggling with addictions, habits, or are trying to heal from trauma. The messages you receive can be trusted to aid you in healing and help you discover your own self But you must believe in yourself.

There are numerous successful healing techniques to choose from and each person is guided to choose the right one for their needs.

Accessing another person's Akashic Record
The akashic file can be thought of as a universal record which records every soul's thought, experience, and act. The record, which was previously available to spiritual masters can now be accessed by anyone anytime and anywhere via various ways of access.

While it can be challenging to gain access to another's Akshic record, it's not impossible. Accessing the akashic records of another is possible when you have the permission of the person who is accessed. Although you aren't able to discover the path of another however, the information you get about the person you access in the records will be based on your own perception of that person and based by your akashic record that is that is related to your journey with the person.

Healing and reading within the Akashic process

To access the akashic records it doesn't require any particular skills. Although certain special skills are helpful Anyone with a spirit is able to connect and gain knowledge. The degree to which you are able to access the information you need depends on the level of your brain's focus, certain individuals are particularly focused on details and most likely get in-depth and complicated information.

The way people receive information can differ. Some people could prefer to be visual or perceive the colors, while others may experience them by listening to melody (sounds) or through dance.

A Pathway Prayer is used to open the records. Akashic records are known as the records. that are opened stay open and stays in your life for the remainder the rest of your existence. As you age and gain more in balance throughout your daily life you'll gain more freedom when you go about removing and entering the Akashic record.

Although the records are accessible to all but some may have difficulties accessing the records or maintaining a balance between the freedom.

Basic healing steps

To determine the healing of the akashic records, one must first master the process of accessing the records. Don't be discouraged when you aren't able to discover what you're seeking. As with any other medium of spiritual development, it will take patience, time and ongoing study to discover this source.

The first step for getting access to the record is to determine what you wish to learn. What is your purpose to look into the record? Perhaps you'd like to find details about your life, or perhaps you want to verify the existence of the record. It's best to know what you're looking for prior to the time.

You can ask a question but keep an eye on the fact that might not always receive an answer.

Set out your goals and ask for guidelines. Make sure you know the reason you wish to gain access to the information.

Give yourself the time to relax your body and mind with any method you prefer to reach a tranquil open, free, and relaxed condition. You can request access to the information related to your query. Try to keep an open, receptive state that lets information be freely absorbed into your consciousness. The knowledge may come in the form of a guide or an angel or auditory, visual or both.

If you make contact with a different creature do not be concerned; simply inquire about their name and then clarify why you're there, and what you're seeking.

Record the experience you had following your session. Even if nothing occurred or you were not able to connect for the recording, you should take time to write down your thoughts, experiences and impressions. It might require more than one try to connect with your Akashic record. It is also possible to get information from your subconscious mind. Find your way back to the right track by using The Akashic records by having an complete knowledge of yourself. The akashic record will assist you in determining the answers to the questions of life or explicit negative beliefs. get rid of the burdens of life and bad habits and make a dramatic change. It also helps you discover your soul's wisdom unlock endless possibilities, re-align your energies, build your inner strength and reconnect to your past lives

A more mindful and conscious lifestyle
The Akashic record links the mind of an individual with the mind of all people. The

mind of an individual is limited to its own experience and thoughts that it may not be able to fully comprehend. Have you ever thought about the reason you do what you do, what makes you're where you're at and why you've encountered certain situations? All that the mind learns is the events that occur throughout its awareness; it is also prone to limited understanding of "why."

Contrary to the universal mind the individual mind is unstable, disoriented and uncertain. Although our universal minds are trustworthy having a strong and well-developed mind is an edge when connecting to an Akashic record.

The Akashic Record is the mind of the universe. Every event that occurs within the universe remains in its record. You are the mind of the universe. Everything about your life's adventures is recorded in its records. The Akashic records link you to the unimaginable aspects of your mind.

There's an entire realm of the universe that's not easily accessed and access to these realms opens up infinite possibilities for your mental, spiritual and physical body. Everything that happens physically stems from the spiritual. Likewise, everything that's visible originates from the un-seen However, as humans we are prone to believe in the things we can perceive and are able to hold onto We usually prefer to stay in the perceived reality. The visible reality is similar to every other piece of the puzzle. The Akashic record assists you in solving these problems. What you can perceive as well as feel, smell, and feel in the world is merely a reflection of your physical being. It is the Akashic record opens your eyes to a higher level of spiritual understanding of lifeand a more profound connection to your inner self and higher self. Experience a spiritual revolution today, discover new and unlimited possibilities, and live a more conscious life.

Power and happiness

It is believed that the Akashic Record is a proven method to find light and truth. It's a wonderful method to understand and comprehend spirituality. The light of the world is Joy Truth is the strength. You have insight into the reality of your life, as well as the reality about your universe in general and how it impacts your personal life.

The mind of every person is searching about something that is not known or undiscovered. Although it might be a mystery but this curiosity exists since the mind believes there is a higher realm that is a higher realm that it needs to be connected to. Any kind of spiritual awakening have been proven to bring about an extreme level of satisfaction and there are numerous accounts of people who claim that they had accessed a portion of themselves that was not there or unresponsive prior to the moment of awakening.

It is a time when people are seeking satisfaction and understand what they really have become as souls. stop the never-ending void that fills your heart , and ever-satisfying curiosity, and fill your body with the knowledge of yourself and the universe it inhabits.

There is nothing more fulfilling than finding the answers to your endless soul-searching.

Everyone is looking to be happy and your happiness will impact every aspect of you and everyone you meet. Happiness is a state happiness that surpasses all other type of emotion. It is the most uplifting as well as the most optimistic emotion. Happiness is an attitude of mind and when you are a happy person you are able to easily take in positive energy; it's an example of the highest quality positive energy.

The universe is open to positive energy and infinite possibilities are open to pure energy. If you're a happy person is a person who lives a true life and can be you and stay honest with your self. Positive thoughts and people can deplete you and sap your positive energy. The balance of your emotions is an important power in the unobserved world and may create the universe in a myriad of ways. Power can bring greater happiness. People who feel strong tend to feel more fulfilled and satisfied in their lives. The less control you have over your power you feel, the less satisfied and less content you'll be.

One connection between happiness and power is satisfaction. The ease of identifying your purpose is based on how content you feel and how much power you have control over. The Akashic record allows you to find the joy within. Make use of your pain to help you find peace, and transform relationships with your universe as well as with yourself. A connection to the Akashic record will open up to you, the universe and you and will help illuminate the entirety of your existence and provide you with an increased sense of purpose.

It is the Akashic record and the claim of your power

Imagine having access to an ebook which teaches all you need to know. Even more amazingly, has the key to altering your life, and reveal unimaginable details about you. Imagine how much more observant and secure your life could be. You shouldn't have to guess at your choices in life; view every step as a way to travel. It is possible to be powerful when you have an understanding of control. The Akashic record allows you to take the ability to control your life, and guides you towards peace within yourself.

Let the healing potential of your soul and increase your awareness. Your soul is the life force inside your body as it keeps your physical body aware. It is essential to believe that the universe is more than what your eyes see, and that the soul is more than what you imagine. You need to believe that you are greater than you imagine and that you were made with a goal You have a reason to live your life for and have many possibilities that must be explored. The power of the soul of yours is a result of how aware you areof yourself, the amount about you that you're conscious of, and how well you are aware of the directions and the patterns of your life's mission. You have to go beyond the physical to reach the highest levels and capacities that your heart has. People have said, "you have no idea how much you can do," however, in many cases, the Akashic record will reveal everything to you. It provides you with a solid understanding of your capabilities as well as a helpful guide to unlocking your potential. The power of the Akashic records is waiting for those who are open to tapping into their endless wisdom. Just open your heart to receive the divine guidance, and you will definitely be blessed with.

The ability to access this Akashic records and power that comes with its knowledge isn't limited to a specific segment or group of people. The record is accessible to anyone who is ready to heal, just as those are willing to explore and discover peace and truth. Be open to a new life. Relax your soul and let the Akashic record come to you.

The Transcending of Your Karmic Patterns
It is believed that we decide our fate prior to our birth by observing a brief glimpse of what our future lives will be like. We can anticipate the way our lives unfold in

terms of our beliefs, culture patterns, habits, and ways of living.

From this perspective we can see the challenges we'll encounter and the barriers to advancing and growing our lives. It is possible to identify instances and circumstances that permit us to experience particular emotions and patterns and difficulties that we haven't been able to go through prior to, adding to this perspective.

Recognizing that we must undergo a part from our lives, regardless of how painful We can begin to discover what transpired through a view of each day as an opportunity balance the balance.

It's hard to discern our karmic tendencies as biases initially. The ego can lead us to believe that we are not responsible for our unique situation. Emancipation as well as redemption are the ultimate goal of Karma. It's still the responsibility of us to determine how much time, energy and effort we will invest in these trends.

We might want to be able to overpower our fate. In that scenario we should think of ourselves as a whole collection of preprogrammed biases such as our genetic heritage gender-specific traits and socialization, as well as the capacity of our brain, psychological background development ancestral roots, the culture and education.

If we aren't able to put our life's events (including repetitions) in perspective with our Karma the real purpose of our life's events (which include cycles) could remain an unknown.

Illusions

The phenomenon of illusion is psychological that is a result of the interaction between practical and logical issues. According to the most common definition, is an inconsistency between the person's perception and a stimuli.

Illusion refers to a misalignment of the senses that may deceive people's perceptions. They can affect any sense however, they can affect the visual sense. (i.e. optical) illusions are among the most understood by scientists.

If you are a viewer and watch an artist perform it can appear as if the magician is doing incredible things. If the ability of a person to motion and depth perception as well as perception are impaired illusions can be seen.

Living in a world of Illusions

The information we have about the world around us is based on our five senses, which are the things we perceive, hear and feel using our eyes, ears and noses, as well as the things we can taste using our tongues. In the end our perception is limited to these five senses. All that we experience, touch, smell or experience outside is just an electrical signal inside our minds. For example we can observe an eagle flying through the sky.

In reality, this sense is a result of an electrical signal inside our brains, not from external sources. We'd never be able to see the eagle again when the sight nerve that connects the brain to it was cut off. This is an electric signal the brain interprets.

Similar to that, whatever you consider as inadequate or not enough as well as sad or happy may disappear and leave no trace. Let's imagine you're sitting in a room and watching television. The brain controls the space. The room is gone when electrical signals that the brain produces concerning it are blocked. The result is that all you can see is a clear desire which seems to be real. It is evident for a time, but then disappears. Once the signal inside the brain returns the image returns.

Living in a world filled with illusions helps you realize that everything is interconnected. The majority of what's right or wrong is stored in your head as a thought. You absorb them and then transmitting them to the world. Every thing has positive and negative elements which allow things to develop and grow. If there's nothing negative, the external world will be troubled and will stop growing since intentional creation is no longer required.

Karma As Opportunity

Sometimes, we're offered an opportunity we believe is just too good to not take advantage of. However, it wouldn't exist without having been brought to us by the karma of our past in connection with our prior desires and effort. It is important to explore these possibilities with determination. We've been working for it in the past, if we could do it in a virtual way. If we expand our horizons today we could be taking the next step in the realization of a potential that is not yet realized. come to.

The effects of Karma aren't always apparent immediately. It's like an unopened, dormant seed. However, at the final, it sprouts, develops and produces fruits. We put your seeds for the next generation in our fertile emotional, physical and mental faculties, and carry the abundant fruit of previous sowings to share with others. Planting is a way to increase the yield of a crop which appears to be sluggish and ineffective.

Karmic Entanglement

Karmic patterns form the basis of our character and identity. Within the omniscient mind Karma is an integral element of our world from the moment of our birth. With our desires for happiness and pleasure as well as the patterns that our families were born into it is hard to get rid of.

Entanglement patterning is a result of karma, similar to what it occurs in microscopic atoms. particle actions cause an interconnected reaction. Each pattern pulls the boundaries of our authentic self. It's like we've lost contact with our real personas. In this dualistic cycle of cause and result the awareness of separation teaches cognition and leads to fragility. We reap what we put into it by way of pleasure and sorrow.

Karma builds up through the ego's conscious actions, doing the same thing over and over again creating karmic patterns that are either positive or harmful. "Repeating the same action with a different outcome" would be the definition for insane. We can anticipate the same results in the event that we don't pay attention to our emotions and act without thinking and don't take the time to learn from our mistakes. We'll be living in a chaotic world until we recognize the patterns of our lives that cause discomfort.

Understanding Family Karma

A lack of a positive connection with your guardians may cause harm. As we get older in our lives, our personality's karmic pattern will be woven into our personality through our relationships with our families and our the society.

The karma of a family member can be very severe. However, it is important to remember that karma may change. Why? Because we hold the dominant power!

Family Karma is a problem we have to deal with as children because of the present circumstances in our families and homes.

Family Karma Is a hallmark of the karmic system that is passed on through the generations. It is passed on over generations. The karmic karma of a family member can affect the ancestors from a similar inheriting family. The karmic actions of our grandparents or parents are often used to determine the karmic nature of the family karma.

We could be incredibly perfect creatures. However, we are suffering from devious parts of our parents as well. Parents could be sick with stomach ulcers. Parents who have been traumatized or neglected accidentally pass these characteristics on to their kids.

We could be spiritual beings. But, we are victimized by evil forces that come from our past. Parents who have been victimized or traumatized, unknowingly pass these characteristics on in their kids.

Family trauma may also be brought back if you don't have an excellent relation with parents. However, there is an option to get out. Children can aid parents to break free from their spiritual conflicts.

Family karma-related symptoms are common among those who have experienced it. The following are some of them:

1. Your family is currently too fragile for you. This could also be part of a pattern.

2. While the family members continue to be a conversation, bizarre conversations within the family might be heard.

3. There could be an emotional reaction or the burden of many obligations at once.

4. You're surrounded by spirituality, which is constantly evolving. The spiritual life is what entices you the most.

Family karma can be partly removed There are methods to fight it. There's no secret formula but forgiveness and appreciation have always influenced or disintegrated family Karma.

Karma and Nation Karma and Nation Karma

We can see how Manu-Samhita (8.304-309) describes how a leader or lord of a nation is awarded one-sixth the absolute fate of the citizens that he is in charge of.

Of course, this is dependent on the individual's entire actions.

Imagine that the majority of people are morally upright and deeply rooted. the ruler helps them keep a peaceful and stable society which they can flourish. In this scenario the lord will participate in the residents of the society's wonderful acts and good karma.

If the monarch doesn't as expected, safeguard and keep pace with the people , but lets hoodlums roam free and create havoc, while paying them for their crimes The general karma of the monarch will be very dark. A tyrant like this will be a victim of his family's displeasure and die in hellfire.

We can observe from the picture that if a ruler is heavily influenced the overall karma of the population, then maybe the future of the nation is shaped by its citizens who's actions are either good or bad. Therefore, no matter what challenges this nation will be facing in the coming years whether it's abundant harvests, a robust economy, or hunger because of drought and famine or victory over our enemies or destruction due to conflict, it'll depend on the way we live our lives today.

Group Karma

The issue about whether there exists "group Karma" occurs from time in the course of time. Are there any possibilities for individuals to have the same karma or is it more of a personal issue?

The karma of another person may hurt nobody but no one is able to profit from the karma of another. However, enormous groups of individuals may end up with essentially identical karma due to making the same misdeeds--accusations, mass massacres, and tortures, and so on. Could this be an instance that is a case of "group theorists"?

Personal Responsibility and Karma

A thorough understanding regarding Karma and the sense of duty it creates is vitally important. But, knowing the responsibility that is entirely yours and what isn't an issue for many.

People who are apprehensive and resentful or trying to carry the burden of the world are destabilizing conditions which many of us have faced at least once in our lives and can result in emotional turmoil and turmoil.

Chapter 8: What Are The Akashic Records?

What we're going to communicate to our brains is related to "Akashic records."

"Akashic Records" represent a symbolic representation which the brain utilizes to symbolize the fact that all thoughts that have ever been thought of exists.

The Akashic Records is the collective consciousness.

It has been described by the name of "Mind of God," which as is believed to be the knowledge or the energetic frequency of all thoughts that has ever been thought about in any universe there existed, ever since the beginning of the division of oneness or Source.

It also includes a little of the future.

What I mean by includes a little bit of the future is that from where you are now there are paths of possibility that extend beyond the time of your life.

"The Future" has always been a vibratory connection to the present.

If you alter your thoughts in the present , the paths in the future are altered.

Then, what is contained within the Akashic Record with regard to the future is just probabilities that stem from your current vibration and where you are in your life right now present moment.

In our human consciousness, we frequently think of this collection of thoughts, we often associate it with libraries since this is what we during our daily lives think of as an information collection.

Therefore, most of the time when people are in those nonlinear dimensions their sensation as being in them is taken away into linear perception.

Therefore, anything that isn't linear is structured in a linear manner by the brain whenever you enter 3D reality.

It's an understanding that is linear after re-entry into the third dimension of consciousness.

The entire experience can be described as sorting through files or images, thereby creating it's like a library of images.

Perhaps you have noticed, you aren't able to find experts in any area to agree.

I'll be discussing the issue in an additional article that will focus on "What you do when everyone is unable to reach an agreement?"

In this issue I'm going to give you information that has never been previously mentioned about Akashic Records as I am not among the people who are in agreement with a lot of the experts so in the area of Akashic Records and their relation to inter-dimensionality are concerned.

Dimensional thinking is one of those things that our brains are occupied with it. It's not something the spirit is concerned about.

However, for the benefit of the brain and for the purpose of explaining Akashic Records, it behooves us to explore the knowledge of the dimensions.

As I mentioned earlier the dimensions are classified according to vibration.

They're not a spatial idea.

The brain is designed to deal with time and space, designed to form wave-functions according to the space and time.

It is saying that dimensions are not present elsewhere than moment.

In reality, all dimensions are over one another within the exact same area.

They are simply different vibrations that are overlapping one over the other.

Therefore, you are present on every dimension at all times.

My opinion is that I believe that the Akashic Records don't correspond to one dimension. Many people believe.

There is generally a consensus on the fact that Akashic Records are on the fifth dimension or something similar to this. However, I don't believe that the information is classified on the same dimension or in another.

The way it functions is that the information is stored on the dimension it is correlated to.

It is possible to imagine the whole Akashic Record in terms of a massive library. Let's say the Akashic Record is Source.

Although right now, you're thinking about libraries it is likely that you are contemplating the possibility of structure.

The reason is that the brain doesn't understand the notion of "no beginning and never ending." Also, it doesn't grasp the idea of "no boundaries".

If we're going to discuss the Akashic Records in general then we must provide the brain with something to connect with.

We can refer to"Source the library. "Source as the Library."

This is the highest level.

The dimensions of the library can be viewed as distinct levels within the library.

Like when you visit the library, there is floor one and floor two. Floor three. . .

The various dimensions could be viewed as levels of the library.

There is also different information regarding each degree.

Thus, each floor of the library is larger than the floor beneath it.

Each floor is a repository of all the information from the floors beneath it and also any new information related to the expansion of consciousness or the vastness of unity consciousness.

To access the Akashic Records is been linked to increasing the frequency of your vibration. In order to make an ideal match for one floor, then to the next floor, and the next floor, and the cycle continues.

Here's an illustration:

Within the 4th dimension the one that is just outside of the third dimension we are able to access every thought that has ever been thought about in connection with the present time, from the moment you were born until your death.

Also, it contains your thoughts, which are basically the self-concept that you hold of yourself This is the reason why, when you exit your body and enter the fourth dimension you'll experience your energy body that is a replica of your energy.

It is an active repetition that is the 3rd dimension, however it is also the fourth dimension is a collection of all thoughts that have ever been considered in relation to the time you live. The third dimension is from present in the moment.

Our brains can imagine four dimensions, and that is the reason we can even have a concept of time.

The third dimension is a time-based reality. This means that all that is real exists right now. . . . . .

Within the 5th dimension each possible timeline, starting from the single point you've selected for your 3D existence, is present.

The symbology that I would like to explain using this symbology is: If has seen the film, "Sliding Doors." In the movie , the character was a victim of a train that she missed. Therefore, the film sets off on two distinct pathways.

In one scenario, she travels on this train and the course of her life is altered according to the circumstances, while on the other one is that she doesn't make the train, and her life continues in the same way.

In this fifth dimension, you can see all of the timelines that are possible on the single option you've picked from any time of your life.

This means that it's that it's not just about the point you are at however, it also includes all possible paths that have been created since the time you were born.

As you can see that this is an enormous amount of information.

The brain of the third dimension is unable to structuring this information for you in a logical manner.

Also, in the timeframe from your first birth until your final death the fifth dimension encompasses all possibilities that exist within that route.

The waves of probabilities in the fifth dimension to create the fourth dimension of a timeline.

This is what you are doing to create your idea of your unique life and the only route that has been chosen by you throughout your physical life.

The sixth dimension you are unbound by space and time which means that you instantly be able to experience a new timeline within the fifth dimension, based on any of the possibilities within the 5th dimension.

Therefore, in a flash, you could shift to the result of what might have happened when something in your early years had been completely altered.

In other words, if one of the possible routes you did not get to take at an initial point, for instance, when that you had been six months of age, then you can follow this until the finish and immediately experience the outcome of the particular probability path.

For the 7th dimension this dimension treated as one point.

Therefore, there is no any more timeframe.

Sixth dimension: a location which all possibilities of timelines within our universe as well as any possible endings for our universe are contained.

They are contained within the single point referred to as Infinity.

Thus every possible timeline that could have or are likely to have cored since the beginning of our universe as a result of the big bang is located inside the seven dimensions.

Thus, everything that ever was thought about the universe is in the seventh dimension.

This is this point that you'd be asking "How do I know if there is greater than Infinity?"

There could be many infinite possibilities.

Other universes are created with different conditions.

When different universes are created in different ways there are laws that apply to this universe.

Therefore, laws differ and laws that are not based on gravity law!

In these universes, and the other infinites the laws may not be identical.

The fundamental laws of nature aren't identical, as the conditions that created those universes are not identical.

In the eighth dimension this is the place where you get access to the infinite relative to the current universe, in relation to the infinite of another universe or even other universes.

The ninth dimension is where, you can access to experience instantly any possibility of any direction at any point being in any universe instantly.

If you're entering the tenth dimension, a lot of us prefer to think of the 10th dimension as the biggest level in the library.

It is, therefore, the highest degree.

What you will encounter in the tenth dimension will be the probabilities of every universe in the ninth dimension.

All of the probabilities for all those universes, within the nineth dimension of space, can be viewed in the present as one point.

Therefore, we might go higher than this.

If you look more than you discover that, you sort of the walls of these libraries, but they're not walls in any way.

Therefore, instead of being levels within the library we now are the library!

The third-dimensional mind to grasp, as I am able to comprehend.

However, when we're outside the tenth dimension, or beyond into the Zero Point Field.

Therefore, in the 10th dimension, all the universes of to the 9th dimension can be considered as one point.

Beyond the 10th dimension, you'll no longer have any points.

What you get is this Zero Point Field which is an ocean of probabilities that we describe as Source.

This is the whole of consciousness collectively that is not the expressions of it.

Therefore, it is essential to be aware that when we explore Akashic Records, most people are talking about the seventh dimension.

It is the frequency of past lives.

That's the sum of all possibilities that can be observed for one soul, starting from its birth in this universe until its final destination within this universe.

It is as a type of energy record, or a seventh-dimensional record of energy.

Therefore, when the majority of people talk about the Akashic Record they are talking about an experience that is seventh-dimensional.

However, I believe it's more important to realize that when we talk regarding The Akashic Record it has many more things than that.

This is just one of the levels of the library you will be able to access.

If you're looking for past life experiences then the "librarian" would advise you to "go into the seventh level," the seventh dimension.

Like everything else it is, you are bound by the beliefs you hold.

In particular, when discussing what is known as the Akashic Record, as you gain access to information contained in the Akashic Record or these frequencies, by becoming a match to the frequencies you are a match.

In order to achieve this, you need to: (a) Believe that they exist; (b) You have to believe that you will reach them; (c) You have to organize your beliefs in a way that allows you to shed the illusion of the third dimension in order to match Akashic records. Akashic record.

It's exactly the same as the saying "You can only be limited by just in your beliefs with regard to the Akashic Records However, you are constrained by your beliefs based on the information you draw from or have a connection to Akashic Record."

Therefore, those who have higher frequencies and higher fit for higher levels of library.

This being said, anyone one of you has access to any time you want to access the Akashic Records. This is the natural consequence of increasing your frequency which is the thing that everyone spiritual beings are talking about.

The more you work to clear the dark areas as you continue to do your shadow work and the more you look toward what you feel comfortable with and you're going to be a good match for more details related with the Akashic Records.

I realize that it could be difficult to comprehend of dimensions because the brain is a tool that is intended to function as an interface for the 3rd dimension.

It is my assurance that the more you meditate and the more work out of the body that you perform and the more you be able to comprehend this idea that your frequency is yours being in tune with your interdimensional universe.

and Akashic Records will become an experience for you, not an idea and that's the thing we're really trying to find.

As soon as it becomes an actual experience to you this knowledge is very real. Then you will be able to access every information that has ever been studied and all thoughts that were ever thought of from the entire universe's beginning in the whole of mass consciousness that is the Source.

How can I access the Akashic Records?
We have previously discussed What are Akashic Records.

In this discussion, we will discuss the topic of How can I Access Akashic Records? Akashic Records?

As we discussed in the our previous chapter In the previous chapter, the Akashic Record is our method of understanding that each thought that has ever been thought exists.

It is still accessible by anyone in any place you're in.

It's not like Akashic Records are located outside of your own.

It's not like there's the Organization in the Universe or a database of information, a location where you can go and then go through it to find the data you're looking for.

The universe is filled with information and information are real vibrations, is in quantum modes.

In other words, there is no actual organization behind it.

In reality, you are interacting in real time with Akashic Records constantly.

If you experience an insight flash whenever you feel like you're accessing intuition, it's because you are connected, throughout the day to Akashic Record, and you can communicate with it.

Everyone can access Akashic Records. Akashic Records.

Finding the information you are looking for from the universe is about tuning your mind to the frequency at which the information is located.

Accessing to the Akashic Records is actually an issue of increasing your frequency of vibration to match an objective view that is not limited by distance, space and time.

I would like to think of it as tuning a radio dial in accordance with the information you want or, more precisely the frequency that you particular desires.

As less tension you have your body, the more frequency will naturally rise as you begin to allow your higher view, the perception from your spiritual self, to be able to flow through your body.

It is essential to be aware of the current resistance.

It is possible to understand the resistance of the radio channel.

Everything in the universe is being ordered to be put into your mind due to the vibration.

The vibrations are constantly being to be matched.

It is only possible to experience the frequency of what's happening to your.

Therefore, to listen to what's broadcast on the radio channel, for instance 99 AM, then you must to tune your radio's channel, first. The dial, which is present within you as a frequency, to the exact frequency.

This is why the resistance appears like it's being tuned to something other than the one you want.

If you tune the frequency of your radio to 99 AM you're at odds with 99 AM.

What exactly is resistance?

It is like holding any thought that is vibrating at a different rate than the your source.

When you're thinking of negative thoughts, that is resistance.

If you find yourself in a state of vibration that is off-balance with what you want, even in the event that it's not already happening, you are being held back by resistance.

You must be within the sound of the answer in order to get the answer.

What does this mean is that when the question you pose but you still have a vibration with the question, and it appears much like a wave of confusion, then you're not compatible with the answer.

To receive an answer to your question from your Akashic Record, you must to place yourself in the realm of vibration: (a) Either having the answer already. Think about what it would be like if you could have that answer and place yourself in that state or (b) it means shifting into a space that is completely allowing or faith in the universe. In other words, you ask an answer and place yourself in a space of open receptivity and there, trusting that you will get the answer.

Both of them are allowable states.

While you can set access to the Akashic Records as a goal, I believe the idea of setting a goal like it is an error.

Most of the time we talk about the abilities of spirituality, such as reaching the Akashic Record, and even being able to leave the body are really just a result of spiritual growth.

That is, when you find harmony between your conscious reality that you live in your individual physical view and the thoughts landscapes that are outside of your physical reality, harmony will create this type of resonance , which will allow you to see this more objective viewpoint that is the place where all of the facts within this universe exists.

If you're focused on confusion, you're blocking your ability to know.

If you're determined to know the truth, you'll allow it to enter your mind as the channel.

The receiving of any data from Akashic Records can be described as channeling and all beings are channels.

You're a channel to the extent that you allow the flow of information through your system.

It is best to imagine it as water flowing through the channel. You repeated, moving yourself into having access to the information you're seeking by opening to allow the channel you wish to gain access to.

It appears that initially you're trying to inform the universe, either through the intention of a question or through an idea which channel you'd prefer to open and the specific details you want to convey.

Then, you let it to be a part of you by permitting it.

What I am referring to by allowing alignment.

You can alter the word"alignment" to enable alignment with spirituality since aligning yourself to the frequency of what you are seeking in order to manifest into something that you experience or a knowing that you have.

Being in a state of trust involves letting go and then thinking about every thought that passes through your mind one that aligns with your needs, seems like being able to allow.

It's all about aligning yourself with what you're looking for.

I'd like to emphasize that when you receive data from Akashic Records, you're in no hurry to change your mind.

Even if you're using off-body work, it's not as if you're heading anywhere.

This perception of travel is an activity your brain performs after re-entry in order to help you to comprehend the experience, since we comprehend things in a 3D way. Otherwise, your brain in the third dimension cannot comprehend what you've just experienced beyond that third dimension.

The heart is, in fact, the most important link between non-physical reality with physical reality.

The information that is emanating via the Akash into the human body, flows through the heart first.

There are numerous studies conducted that involve a person being connected to devices that record brain activity as well as the body.

Additionally, there are images that are picked at random by computers and then flashed in front of people. So there is no way of knowing which image will be released the next.
There are scary images interspersed with images that could create feelings of security within humans, as well as enjoyable things, and there's nobody who can tell the viewer to predict what's going to happen next.